Introduction to the Libertarian Party

For Democrats, Republicans, Libertarians, Independents, and Everyone Else

Wes Benedict

ISBN-13: 978-1489501769
ISBN-10: 1489501762

I dedicate this book to the thousands of Libertarian Party candidates, officers, and other activists who have generously volunteered their time and talents to promote liberty in America without expecting anything in return beyond the satisfaction of having done what they think is right. I also thank our family members, like my wife Andrea, for their support.

CONTENTS

ACKNOWLEDGMENTS

I want to thank Arthur DiBianca for his tremendous editing work. This book would not have been possible without his help.

INTRODUCTION

HOW I FOUND THE LIBERTARIAN PARTY

I used to stay up late, night after night, arguing with the same old friends about politics.

The later it got, the drunker we got, and the louder we got. Usually we had fun, and sometimes we got mad. But the one thing we absolutely *never* did was change each others' minds.

I finally came to my senses. After one heavy six-month period of arguing, I realized I had changed zero minds. If I wanted to change the world in my lifetime, I would have to find a faster way.

Eventually, I did: I found the Libertarian Party (LP), solidified my political views, and became one of the top Libertarian Party activists in the nation. My experience as a Libertarian Party member, volunteer, candidate, employee, and party officer at the local, state, and national levels helps me give this complete introduction to the Libertarian Party from an insider's perspective.

But back then, before finding the LP, I actually decided I would have to start a *new country* to prove that my political views were right!

In 1996 I was starting an MBA at the University of Michigan. I was also starting to think about government policies more than ever.

I was obsessed.

Republicans and Democrats always blamed each other for every problem. Take the deficit. When Ronald Reagan was president, Republicans blamed the deficit on welfare and pork projects supported by Democrats.

Meanwhile, Democrats blamed it on Reagan's military spending.

In a country where Republicans and Democrats alternate control pretty frequently, and no one is in charge for long, it was hard for me to tell which party causes problems like the deficit. I was thinking they both did, and probably nothing was going to change.

Being an engineer with a scientific mindset, I figured the only way to prove freedom works was to start a new country, perhaps a benevolent dictatorship, where freedom was guaranteed.

I remember at one point I actually thought I ought to drop out of the MBA program and present a business plan to some venture capitalists for starting my new country.

The fundamentals involved buying cheap land from a poor country, instituting a constitution that truly protected freedom, and reaping the profits as the land value skyrocketed, like it had in Hong Kong and Singapore. (Now don't get me wrong: Hong Kong and Singapore have horrible civil liberties records, and are far from being libertarian, but they do have really valuable real estate.)

In any case, I was thinking that the *only way* to change the world was to start a new country.

Was I insane? Surely someone had thought of that before! Even if my idea was sound, could I pull it off? What would all the laws be in this new country?

Then I stumbled upon the Libertarian Party.

Finally, a group of people with principles just like mine, right here in America! And they had a plan to change the world!

Much to my relief, I didn't have to start from scratch, drop out of graduate school, and start a whole new country. I could apply my efforts to building the Libertarian Party right here, right now.

PART I
THE PHILOSOPHICAL SIDE

CHAPTER 1

DON'T HIT PEOPLE AND DON'T TAKE THEIR STUFF

Don't hit people and don't take their stuff. I didn't coin that phrase, but it pretty much sums up libertarianism.

Soon after joining the Libertarian Party I picked up a book by Dr. Mary J. Ruwart, a scientist and Libertarian Party activist. The book was called *Healing Our World: The Other Piece of the Puzzle*. It introduced me to a lot of the concepts in this chapter.

Let me start with "Don't take their stuff."

Most of us know it's wrong to walk next door and steal something from a neighbor.

Now, what if we hire a gang to steal something from the neighbor? Of course you probably still think that would be wrong.

Now, how about if we get together with all the neighbors on the block and *vote* to steal something from that neighbor? Of course that neighbor will still get a vote (because we believe in democracy), but he'll probably be outvoted, and then we get his stuff.

Does that still sound wrong?

Well unfortunately, that's the essence of government and taxation.

People get together, and instead of hiring a gang of criminals to take your stuff, they use a voting process and call it the government. And you have to pay whatever taxes they demand, or they'll threaten you, and if necessary follow up with gun-toting enforcers to hit you and take your stuff.

It's not like a health club, where people voluntarily choose to join and agree to pay dues. With government, you just have to pay, period.

Most people feel it's wrong to steal from their neighbors, just like they learned when they were children. But when you use the government as an intermediary, suddenly they're comfortable with it.

Libertarians believe taxation is still theft, even if a lot of people voted on it and someone wrote on a piece of paper that it's a legal law.

Now on to the "Don't hit people" part.

We all know it's wrong to just walk next door and beat up your neighbor. Similarly, we know it's wrong to hire a thug or a hit man to beat up your neighbor or murder him. But what if we form a government and pass a law saying you have to behave a certain way, or we'll hit you?

Government force isn't just used to take stuff. It's also used to make people behave a certain way. In some countries, governments prohibit certain religions like Christianity, and will imprison or kill people if they disobey. In America, we used to prohibit interracial marriage. We still throw people in jail if they smoke marijuana. The rules and penalties are made up by government, often (but not always) with the consent of the majority. Those rules and penalties get imposed on you whether you personally consent to them or not. If you break a rule, the government will tell you to stop and will threaten you. And if you refuse to stop, policemen will make you stop by hitting you and dragging you to jail.

Libertarians think it's wrong to hit people for behavior that doesn't hurt anyone else, even if a lot of people voted on it and wrote on a piece of paper that the behavior is prohibited.

History is full of examples of heroic people refusing to obey their government, from Jesus Christ disobeying the Romans, to the American Revolutionaries, to people who helped Jews escape from Nazi Germany. Sometimes you get away with disobeying government, and sometimes you don't. Most of us think it's wrong to disobey government, but most of us also have some exceptions.

Libertarians think the role of government should be to protect our lives, liberty, and property. We want the government to stop thieves and murderers. We don't want the government to *be* a bunch of thieves and murderers.

Libertarians support the non-aggression principle: **No one should initiate force against others**. (We're not pacifists though—responding to force in self-defense is okay.)

"Don't hit people and don't take their stuff." Most of us learned that as children, and we still hold to it as adults. But somehow, we abandon it when we delegate the enforcement to government.

The Libertarian Party is the party of principle, and we want to move towards a society where government respects the non-aggression principle.

I don't want to spend too much time discussing the theories behind libertarianism. A few seconds of searching on the Internet will reveal thousands of books and articles that do an extensive job of that. This book is an introduction to the Libertarian Party, primarily geared towards potential recruits and new activists, so I don't want to get too deep into theory. But I wanted to give a quick overview of libertarianism, so that if you become a Libertarian Party political activist, you'll have a good sense of what it is.

When you join the Libertarian Party, you are asked to sign a pledge that says *I certify that I oppose the initiation of force to achieve political or social goals.* If you agree with that, please don't vote for people who want to hit people and take their stuff!

CHAPTER 2

WHAT IS A LIBERTARIAN?

If I'm talking to someone who might have never heard of the Libertarian Party, I'll often say, "You got the Republicans and Democrats, and in a distant third are the Libertarians." Then I'll go on to explain that Libertarians are for free markets and low taxes like Republicans, but we're also for civil liberties and personal freedoms like Democrats. For example, we're for free speech and okay with gay marriage. We're for freedom on every issue. Then I'll ask them to take the World's Smallest Political Quiz (Chapter 10), because it's the best way I've found to get someone to quickly understand what a libertarian is.

At this point I should mention that, while Republicans usually claim they're for smaller government, they're really not. And while Democrats claim they support personal freedoms, they really don't. Republican and Democratic hypocrisy earned whole chapters in this book.

A libertarian is simply someone who supports liberty.

The Merriam-Webster dictionary defines libertarian (with a small "l") as "an advocate of the doctrine of free will; a person who upholds the principles of individual liberty especially of thought and action." It goes on to define Libertarian with a capital "L" as "a member of a political party advocating libertarian principles."

You can have libertarian views without being a member of the Libertarian Party, just like you can be a liberal without being a member of the Democratic Party.

The capital "L" is sometimes a helpful distinction. When I capitalize the word Libertarian in this book, I am referring to a Libertarian Party member or Libertarian Party candidate. But when I use the lower case "libertarian" I'm referring to someone who supports the libertarian philosophy, whether or not the person is also a capital-L Libertarian. (When it's at the start of a sentence, you can't always tell which one it is, but it usually doesn't matter.)

Libertarians have used many slogans over the years to describe themselves. Several examples are:

1) Fiscally conservative, socially liberal
2) More freedom, less government
3) We're pro-choice on everything
4) Minimum government, maximum freedom
5) Free markets, civil liberties, and peace

Libertarians believe you should be able to do whatever you want with yourself and your property, as long as you aren't hurting others. Live and let live!

The government we want is one that protects your rights, not one that tries to give you stuff or tell you how to live your life. To quote Thoreau, "That government is best which governs least."

Libertarianism is a consistent philosophy. You don't have to memorize the Libertarian Party platform or any other long document to know the libertarian position on an issue. You can usually figure it out on your own. Whatever the issue, we favor less government, or even no government involvement.

We believe that in most cases, government makes things worse and freedom makes things better. Libertarians can usually back that up with empirical studies.

However, giving the "utilitarian" argument—that a libertarian approach *works* better—is not enough for most libertarians, who would go further and say that freedom is just plain right. People should be free. They have a right to be free. They don't need a justification for being free. To quote the Declaration of Independence, "We hold these truths to be self-evident, that all men are created equal, that they are endowed by their Creator with certain unalienable Rights, that among these are Life, Liberty, and the pursuit of Happiness."

Libertarians believe that free markets are the best way to create wealth, unrestricted voluntary trade is the best way to distribute wealth, and a society where people are free to act (without violating the rights of others) is the only society where they can exhibit virtuous behavior.

Libertarians are black, white, young, old, straight, gay, Christian, atheist, yuppie, hippie, vegetarian, hamburger lovers, rich, poor, conservative, liberal, greedy, generous, eccentric, and just plain average.

What do libertarians agree on? Actually, very little. They agree to disagree, and they want a government that lets them do that. Therefore, as libertarians, they agree that the only legitimate role of government is to protect people's rights: their personal and economic freedom.

Libertarians believe minimal government will result in the best society for all people to live in. It will not be a utopia free of disease, poverty, crime, and other problems. Utopias are impossible. But most libertarians want to make things better, for themselves and for other people.

Libertarians believe that every person should be able to decide where to attend school, what to believe, what to say, who to associate with, what to eat, and what to buy. But you're not allowed to steal anything, and you need to deal with the consequences of your choices.

Libertarians believe you own yourself, and you are personally responsible for yourself. That doesn't mean you must live all by yourself and pay for everything yourself, and if you are poor, sick, or disabled you're out of luck and must suffer in poverty or die. But instead of government charity or welfare, we think poor and disabled people should rely on *voluntary* charity from family, friends, strangers, or private charitable organizations and churches.

Voluntary charity may sound far-fetched at first. But it's happening around us all the time. One spouse stays home while the other gets a paying job. People take care of their children or sick parents. Friends let unemployed friends live on the couch temporarily. The number of private organizations and personal relationships that involve charity are too large to count. A hundred years ago, government was much smaller in the U.S., and nearly all charity was private.

We don't deny that some people could fall through the cracks. But many people fall through the cracks even with a well-intentioned big-government safety net. Plenty of people get sick, get hurt, or have other bad things happen to them even though there are many government policies and government employees trying to stop those things.

Many studies show that more people suffer poverty in places where government is big, than places where government is small.

Sometimes the word "libertarian" evokes the rugged individualistic image of a strong, capable, self-reliant person (usually male) with plenty of guns and ammo in the woods away from civilization, growing his own food, and perhaps paranoid that government satellites or drones are spying on him. (Not that there's anything wrong with rugged individualists.) But being libertarian does not require being independent from other people. Libertarians expect relationships, dependencies, and communities to develop. But libertarians support a society where *voluntary* relationships and associations can form, rather than government-imposed relationships.

For example, we oppose government schools because those are forced relationships between people who must pay taxes, and children who must go to the school they are assigned by the government. On the other hand, we support the right of free people to form schools, clubs, churches, insurance associations, issue advocacy groups, or anything else.

America is one of the most libertarian countries on earth (or maybe *least un-libertarian*), so that's good news for Americans. But it's far from perfect. Some things have gotten more libertarian over time, like ending slavery, and allowing gays to come out of the closet without worrying about criminal prosecution. On the other hand, many things have gotten less libertarian. In 1912, there was no federal income tax. Now we pay rates up to 40%.

The United States Constitution is a fairly libertarian document. Of course it contained terrible exceptions, like allowing slavery, which is the opposite of libertarian. And the Constitution still provides for a government post office and an income tax, things libertarians would get rid of. But by and large, our government would be a whole lot smaller if our politicians followed the Constitution.

Unfortunately, the meaning of the Constitution has been perverted to allow for a huge amount of government that the Constitution was intended to prevent.

Libertarians would like to shrink the federal government so that it complies with the Constitution, and then continue shrinking it further. We'd also shrink state and local governments.

Libertarians believe the government should only do what's needed to protect our rights: provide for the national defense, provide police, courts, and jails, and help enforce contracts. And plenty of those functions could be quite small, perhaps privatized, or even dispensed with in some cases. For example, there are contracts calling for private arbitration instead of using the government's courts; you've certainly seen private security guards; and you've dared to go outside the city limits—where no city government is in force!

While libertarian ideas have been around perhaps forever, the Libertarian Party was founded in 1971. The Libertarian Party is America's third-largest political party. It is the only party dedicated to freedom on every issue. Many Libertarians serve in elected office throughout the U.S., and there are Libertarian Party organizations in all 50 states. We run hundreds of candidates for election every two years, for everything from President and Congress down to state legislatures and local offices. It's great when we win elections and can implement libertarian policies directly. But, whether we win or lose elections, every vote for a Libertarian helps the cause.

The purpose of the Libertarian Party is to nominate candidates for public office and help them get elected, in order to move public policy in a libertarian direction.

CHAPTER 3

LIBERTARIANS ON 25 ISSUES

Throughout this book I'll be giving the libertarian position on various issues. I should point out that these are my opinions about what the libertarian position is. Plenty of people may disagree with my interpretations or conclusions.

Ernest Hancock, a libertarian activist and founder of libertarian website *Freedom's Phoenix*, is famous for summing up libertarian positions with his saying: "Freedom is the answer. What's the question?"

Libertarianism is a consistent philosophy, so it's pretty easy to figure out the libertarian position on a particular issue, even if you haven't heard it discussed by libertarians before.

Whatever the issue, libertarians support maximum freedom and minimum government. Libertarians can often explain how society would be better off that way, and offer concrete data to back it up.

Since practically every issue you can think of, from taxes to jails, is written about extensively, I'm not going to try to explain or defend the libertarian positions in detail in this book. You can research any issue and find tons of information about the libertarian perspective.

If it's an issue I want to know a lot about, I usually start at the Cato Institute.

In any case, below are brief descriptions of the libertarian position on 25 issues.

Taxes. Libertarians would eliminate taxes or lower taxes as much as possible, and we'd cut spending as well, by reducing services and eliminating programs. Plenty of studies show countries with lower taxation have better overall economies than countries with higher taxation. Which is greedier: to want to keep your own money, or to want to take someone else's through taxation?

Civil Liberties. Libertarians support civil liberties and oppose legislation like the so-called Patriot Act, which gives the government power to spy on Americans without a warrant, or arrest them and hold them without a trial.

Terrorism. America's aggressive foreign policy causes resentment and leads to terrorism. We should stop intervening in places like the Middle East. We'd experience less terrorism.

Free markets. Libertarians support free markets. We don't have free markets today. Our system in the U.S. is partially free, but horribly perverted with regulations, high taxes, loopholes, and subsidies. Often, Big Business supports regulations in order to hurt their competitors and help themselves. Or they push for special handouts. For example, agribusiness Archer Daniels Midland lobbies and gets subsidies for its corn processing activities. That's called "corporate welfare," and libertarians are against it.

Free speech. Absolutely! Prohibit any speech you want on your private property, but leave others alone. So yes, your place of employment, church, or private school might prohibit certain speech on their property, but they shouldn't impose their policies on their neighbors. Government should not prohibit or restrict speech.

Socialism. Libertarians oppose socialism at the government level. However, if a group of individuals want to form a commune or live together and have joint ownership of things, that's fine.

Free trade. People have the right to trade with each other, and international free trade benefits everyone involved. Even if other countries refuse to trade freely, America is still better off unilaterally practicing free trade and eliminating tariffs, quotas and other trade barriers.

Free health care. Libertarians support a free *market* in health care, but not government-provided free health care. You should not be forced to pay for other people's health care. And it turns out, government lowers the quality of health care and drives up the costs.

Drugs. Libertarians would end prohibition of substances like marijuana. The war on drugs does more harm than good, and it's a violation of people's freedom to do whatever they want, so long as they're not hurting others. As with alcohol, if you drive and kill someone, then you are hurting someone else and libertarians obviously oppose that. Private entities like schools, businesses, and individuals should set their own policies for drug use and/or drug testing instead of leaving this matter up to the government.

Privatization. If you mean "get the government out of it," libertarians probably agree. However, libertarians aren't too interested in "outsourcing" government activities (while still paying for them with taxes). Libertarians usually want government to stop doing those activities altogether.

Social Security. What a big mistake starting this program was. It's just intergenerational theft. Even worse, it's basically a Ponzi scheme that causes each generation to feel more abused than the last.

Welfare. Libertarians oppose government welfare. It's wrong to force some people to pay for the support of others, and welfare corrupts people's motivation. A strong economy is much better for poor people than welfare. Private organizations and individuals are best at determining who truly needs help, and they generally encourage behavior that leads toward self-sufficiency.

Labor unions. Any group has the right to assemble and take peaceful action. Employers have the right to hire or fire or expel from private property whomever they please. Initiation of violence by either group is wrong.

Guns. Hunting is not the issue. The "right to bear arms" was intended to provide people the capacity to protect themselves, whether it's from criminals or from a government that attacks its citizens. Contrary to what you hear, crime actually drops when gun ownership increases. Libertarians respect the right of citizens to hunt on private property where owners allow it.

Federal Reserve. Libertarians don't like the Fed and want to get rid of it. It has the power to manipulate currency supplies and interest rates, and often causes inflation. Libertarians support a free market in currencies.

Military. Our soldiers should be well equipped to protect Americans in America, but that's it. We have soldiers in over 100 foreign countries. What if 100 countries had soldiers in America? Our excessive intervention in foreign countries' affairs creates resentment, attracts terrorism, and wastes hundreds of billions of dollars each year.

Education. Government schools are monopolies that cost double what private schools cost, often teach viewpoints that many parents don't like, and generally provide an inferior education. Libertarians want the government to get out of the education business. Some libertarians suggest that we start with tax credits and/or vouchers for private schools, but the ideal is "total separation of school and state."

Environment. Most Americans care about the environment. Did you ever notice how it's the government-owned property that is the most polluted? Who owns the lakes, rivers, roadsides, and most air emission rights? Eliminate the EPA and treat pollution like a trespass. Market-oriented reforms will provide a cleaner environment at lower costs.

Monopolies. Only the government has sponsored successful monopolies that have treated consumers poorly, like the Post Office, utilities, and schools. The 19th-century "robber barons" are a myth. They actually reduced prices drastically and expanded services rapidly. They only hurt consumers when they enlisted the government to prevent competition. Repeal antitrust laws, licensing laws, and trade barriers that protect special interests.

Regulations. Regulations are supposed to help order the economy and protect consumers from dangerous products. Much existing regulation is voluntary and private, enforced by associations and third parties, such as Underwriters Laboratories, kosher foods, Consumer Reports, Standard & Poor's, and seals of approval. Regulatory functions should be re-privatized to promote innovation, reduce costs, and allow individuals to choose not to follow regulations they deem harmful to themselves. Get rid of most government regulations.

Gambling and prostitution. Gambling and prostitution should be legal everywhere. I'm not saying they're smart things to do, but when a person gambles, he or she does not violate anyone else's rights. Ditto for prostitution. As Lysander Spooner said, "Vices are not crimes."

Immigration. It should be *easy* for foreigners to come work legally in the U.S. Right now, our laws make it almost impossible.

Farm subsidies. Get rid of them, period.

Foreign aid. End foreign aid to all countries.

Minimum wage. There should be no minimum wage. It's wrong to dictate to employees and employers what rates they have to agree on. And the minimum wage interferes with the economy and increases unemployment.

CHAPTER 4

WHAT DOES A LIBERTARIAN GOVERNMENT LOOK LIKE?

The short answer is "very small."

The Declaration of Independence talks about our "unalienable rights," and says that "to secure these rights, governments are instituted." I think that indicates where most libertarians stand. To the extent that government force is justifiable, it must be used specifically to secure individual rights. When police find and arrest a murderer, they are helping to secure individual rights. But when the Social Security Administration takes money from young people and hands it to old people, that has nothing to do with individual rights. (But I don't want to spend too much time defining "rights"—there are plenty of books about that.)

Most libertarians think government should provide these basic services:

- A small police force (to help protect people from violence and other crimes of aggression)
- Courts of law
- A small military to defend from invasion

Note all the things that government would not be doing: education, health care, Social Security, welfare, foreign wars, drug prohibition, food inspections, occupational licensing, zoning, air traffic control, mail delivery, unemployment benefits, farm subsidies, trade barriers, work regulations, power generation, etc., etc.

Libertarians disagree about how much those basic services should be funded by taxes. Some libertarians think it's okay to do it all with taxes. Some libertarians want to fund it partially through voluntary donations. Some libertarians think taxation should be illegal, and the government should only be as big as the amount of voluntary funding it can obtain.

To sum it up, I'd say that some libertarians want a government that's 10% as powerful as it is now; some would prefer 1%; and a few would prefer 0%. So I think it's safe to say that most libertarians want to cut the power and expense of government by at least 90%, and that's obviously a very long way from the status quo.

CHAPTER 5

ARE LIBERTARIANS TOO EXTREME?

A famous politician once said, "Extremism in the defense of liberty is no vice." (He also liked having a gigantic taxpayer-funded military. Nevertheless, I like the quote.)

Compared to the status quo, I think it's fair to say that libertarianism is extreme. But obviously I don't think it's *too* extreme.

When people hear the libertarian point of view, they sometimes think it sounds like a fantasy world that could never really exist. (No public schools? That's *impossible!*) However, almost every policy that libertarians propose is currently in use somewhere in the world, or has been in the past.

Legalize prostitution? Well, prostitution is basically legal in parts of Nevada and Europe. Even where it's illegal, many places have black markets that customers know about and the police quietly ignore.

Legalize drugs? Well, marijuana is for all practical purposes legal in Holland, and Portugal recently legalized most drugs. The states of Colorado and Washington legalized the possession and sale of marijuana in 2012.

While the United States has a huge military and constantly gets involved in foreign conflicts, many other countries like Switzerland and Costa Rica stay out of foreign wars. They save lots of money and they don't seem to be too worried about terrorism.

Does free trade sound extreme? We have free trade between Texas and New York. I don't think most Texans and New Yorkers are angry about that. Why not have free trade between countries? Some people worry that free trade between rich and poor countries would make the rich countries poor—or the poor countries poorer—but studies show that rich and poor people both benefit from free trade. After all, we have free trade between rich people and poor people in Los Angeles and every other city. Many countries have low tariffs or no tariffs, like Hong Kong and Sweden, and usually the lower the trade barriers, the wealthier the country's citizens. Actually, the United States also has relatively low tariffs on most products. America has free trade in a lot of ways; I think most Americans just don't realize it.

Can you imagine free speech? I'm not just talking about the right to say unpopular things—I'm talking about going further and allowing outright lies! That's basically how the Internet and email work. Spam emails claiming to be from the Ivory Coast or Nigeria constantly lie to us and ask for our bank account numbers. Yet somehow we learn to survive and even thrive with a wildly open Internet. We've figured out that we shouldn't just believe anything anyone tells us.

Income tax? In 1910 there was no federal income tax, but the American economy was growing rapidly. People from all over the world wanted to come to the U.S.

Welfare? Before government welfare, people relied on their families and private charity, or got off their butts and did some work even if it made their back hurt.

When it comes to education, road-building, or many issues, it's hard for people to imagine how it could work without the government involved. People living under communism probably couldn't imagine getting food if the government stopped providing it. But just because it's hard to imagine, doesn't mean it can't happen. It mostly means we haven't tried. The world has a rich history of private roads, private transit, and private education, and there are thousands of research papers examining how we could move towards those things now.

Libertarianism may well be extreme—I think it would be extremely beneficial! However, the government we have today is not only anti-libertarian, it's moving steadily towards authoritarianism. I bet if George Washington or Thomas Jefferson knew how big and intrusive our government has become, they would be horrified. (And they would be surprised when people called them extremists.) Throughout history, authoritarianism has proven to be harmful to life, liberty, and happiness. America needs a strong dose of extreme libertarianism.

CHAPTER 6

REPUBLICAN HYPOCRITES

Republicans usually go around saying they want "less government." That kind of sounds like Libertarians, right?

Would Republicans end the war on drugs, end mandatory Social Security and Medicare, repeal the Patriot Act, bring our troops home from around the world, and slash the military budget?

Of course they wouldn't. (But Libertarians would.)

What's even more amazing is how often Republicans work to massively expand government.

Let's look at a few examples: Mitt Romney, John McCain, George Bushes I and II, those new Tea Party Republicans, and that conservative icon: President Ronald Reagan.

Read my lips: "Ronald Reagan grew government much more than Bill Clinton." That's not what you hear every day, but it's true. Do the research yourself if you don't believe me, and if you're a Republican, feel free to come up with all kinds of excuses. If you can't handle the truth, I can't make you. Some conservatives will admit that Presidents George Bush (I and II) grew government, but they hold up Reagan as a government-cutting ideal.

In real life, Ronald Reagan signed one gigantic spending bill after another. During his administration, military spending grew a ton, but nothing else got cut, so overall spending went way up. Reagan boosted import tariffs and trade restrictions. Reagan cut marginal income tax rates—but he also raised Social Security taxes. Reagan increased farm subsidies. Federal spending under Reagan grew from $678 billion to $1.14 trillion.

And here's the amazing thing: when you measure federal spending as a percentage of GDP, the Reagan administration had the *highest spending in American history*. I'm not making that up. The Obama administration is likely to beat him though. (If you're a Reagan lover, maybe you can brag about that.)

Have I offended you yet by accusing Ronald Reagan of growing the government?

I used to worry about offending people. Back when I was executive director of the Libertarian Party, whenever I pointed out Reagan's government growth, quite a few people would complain to me. They'd tell me not to attack Reagan because he was so popular. Finally I set up a poll and asked Libertarian readers this question: "How should Libertarians deal with the myth that Ronald Reagan reduced government?" Sixty percent said, "Libertarians should point out that Reagan grew government." Only eight percent said, "Don't bring it up, to avoid offending his fans."

I'm not just pointing out that Reagan grew government for the shock value. If Reagan and other Republicans actually had a track record of cutting government, that could hurt the case for having a Libertarian Party. But the fact remains, Republicans almost always have grown government, and often even faster than Democrats.

I don't know what it is that lets people so readily ignore reality. But I admit, it happened to me as well! Before I was a Libertarian, I hated Bill Clinton's guts, and I loved Ronald Reagan. In fact, I don't think I was able to admit that Reagan grew government faster than

Clinton until ten years *after* becoming a Libertarian.

Now I think President Bill Clinton may have been the best president in my lifetime! (I was born at the end of Lyndon B. Johnson's term.) That doesn't mean I think he was a good president. I just don't think he achieved as much bad stuff as the others— maybe he was too embroiled in scandals to get as much done.

Let's give some more recent examples of Republicans growing government, and then go backwards in time to the founding of the Libertarian Party in 1971.

The 2012 Republican nominee for president, Mitt Romney, started a healthcare program known as RomneyCare while he was Massachusetts Governor. It became the framework for Obamacare.

Remember the Tea Party? The huge Tea Party protests of 2009 were in response to the bailouts offered by Republican President George W. Bush, and passed with the help of Republicans. In fact, the 2008 Republican presidential nominee, John McCain, is famous for suspending his campaign so he could rush back to Washington to vote for the Troubled Asset Relief Program (TARP) bailout bills.

The Tea Party helped kick out some incumbent Republicans in 2010, and replaced them with new Tea Party Republicans. But when it came around to the budget fights in 2011, most of the "Tea Party Congressmen" voted for deals that increased federal spending once again. Of course, those Tea Party Republicans made all kinds of excuses for going along with spending increases. With only a few exceptions, that's what Republicans in Congress do.

The 2012 Republican vice presidential nominee, Paul Ryan, was held up as a "budget hawk." Perhaps by Republican standards he's a budget hawk, but in reality he has a horrible voting record. Ryan voted for the TARP bailouts, the Chrysler and GM bailouts, "No Child Left Behind," the 2003 prescription drug Medicare expansion, and ethanol subsidies. In fact, Paul Ryan's budgets always kept federal spending higher than it was under Clinton! (I'm talking percentage of GDP.)

A lot of Republicans complained about President Obama's 2009 stimulus plans, but President Bush had his own 2008 stimulus plan, mailing $300 and $600 "rebate" checks to individuals and families throughout the U.S., and Republicans supported it.

I think President George W. Bush's worst offenses were the wars in Iraq and Afghanistan, which will cost trillions of dollars when all is said and done. He also supported the Patriot Act, which not only cost money, but also gave the government more power to violate our rights.

Back in the 1990s, I was excited by Newt Gingrich and the "Contract with America." But Republicans never actually supported eliminating any federal departments. Newt later became sort of famous for presenting wacky new ideas for government programs.

Of course, perhaps the most classic failure was the senior President George H. W. Bush. "Read my lips: no new taxes." I don't have to remind you that Bush reneged on his promise and signed new taxes into law. (I voted for Ross Perot in 1992. That was before I knew about the Libertarian Party. Not that Ross Perot was a libertarian.)

You can find plenty of examples at the state and local levels of Republicans growing government. For one thing, many states have Republican governors and Republican-controlled legislatures, but their budgets always go up faster than inflation plus population growth.

Texas is a good example, and I have more familiarity with Texas politics than other states. Republican Governor Rick Perry and the Republican legislature instituted a new tax on business revenue in 2006. Rick Perry also secured a $300 million dollar business handout slush fund that he and the two leaders of the legislature could dole out to whomever they chose. That's corporate welfare, a recipe for corruption, and it's as bad as the TARP bailouts. In fact, Rick Perry gave $20 million dollars to Countrywide Financial—which later went bankrupt.

Texas Republicans supported creating a new $3 billion Texas taxpayer-funded medical research center.

Rick Perry signed an executive order hoping to force young Texas schoolgirls to get the HPV vaccine even if it was against their parents' will—meanwhile, his former chief of staff was a lobbyist for Merck, which made the vaccine.

You can find examples of Republicans growing government throughout the U.S. at the state and local levels. An easy way to prove it to yourself is to pick any county that has been controlled by Republicans for the last four years. Look at the county budget today versus four years ago. Feel free to factor in inflation and population growth. Did spending grow? I bet it did!

I also want to mention Republican President Richard Nixon, because he helped inspire the Libertarian Party.

Back in 1971, the American economy was looking weak, and Nixon had a great idea: institute wage and price controls! (How "free market"!) And as a bonus, he decided to take the U.S. dollar completely off the gold standard. Those actions made some free market-loving activists so mad, they decided to found the Libertarian Party.

Going back to 1971, I can't think of one significant government program that Republicans have gotten rid of—not one.

I know that some Republicans reading this chapter will just refuse to believe that Republicans don't want to cut government. Well, I can't do much more than state the facts. I guess some people will just believe what they want to.

Since Republicans don't want to cut government, why do they pretend so much? I'm not totally sure. I think it's mostly to make themselves sound different from Democrats. (It's important to create the illusion of a huge battle between two opposite sides who don't agree on anything.)

It might also be because many Republican voters have the same attitude—they want to cut government in their imaginations, but not in real life.

CHAPTER 7

DEMOCRATIC HYPOCRITES

So Democrats don't support free markets, but at least they care about the poor, and they want to protect our civil liberties, right?

Wrong.

Should the government subsidize luxury stores that sell $46 men's underwear? I don't think so. That's why I helped to fight against a $60 million subsidy for a high-end mall that sells luxury items in Austin, Texas.

The city and county governments in Austin, Texas are dominated by Democrats, and every single Democrat voted to subsidize the mall despite lots of outcry against it. After the mall was built, a group of us tried to pass an initiative to overturn the subsidy.

I visited the mall to check it out. Inside the Neiman Marcus (an upscale clothing store), I came across a pair of underwear for $46. That seemed like an absurdly high price for men's underwear, but I decided I just had to have it. I pinned it on a poster board and brought it to a hearing at the Austin City Council to help explain why I was against the mall.

I told the city council it was wrong to give a $60 million subsidy to a mall where rich people shop, while poor people had to shop at regular malls or stores that had to pay full tax rates. (Search the Internet for "$46 Underwear Fighting $60 Million Domain Mall Subsidies" for a video of my delivery to the city council.) Some called my presentation hilarious, others said it was over the top. Unfortunately, on election day we lost 52% to 48%.

Democrats often talk about helping the poor, but often the actions they take help the rich instead of the poor. Corporate welfare like "economic development subsidies" is just one of many ways Democrats hurt the poor.

Another much smaller example is subsidies for the arts. Democrats love those. The problem is, when you think about it, why should poor people pay higher taxes so rich people can get cheaper tickets to the opera?

One of the worst things Democratic hypocrites have done is support the war on drugs. America has the highest incarceration rate in the world and many people are in jail on drug-related charges.

Democrats say they want to help minorities, but the war on drugs hurts minorities badly. Minorities are far more likely to be thrown in jail for drug use than whites. Black market inner-city violence is brutal. People who get convicted of a nonviolent drug felony have their lives ruined. They'll never be able to get a job, so all they can do is go back to drug trafficking. And all of us (including poor people) have to pay higher taxes to support all the police, prosecution, and prisons. Meanwhile, the wealthy contractors who build prisons, and the wealthy lawyers, and everyone else involved in the criminal justice system profit. Thanks, Democrats!

And of course, the war on drugs doesn't just hurt the poor, it also hurts our civil liberties. A whole lot of intrusive laws have been upheld as constitutional (when they're obviously not) because judges have said they are needed for the war on drugs. I'm talking about things like highway checkpoints, no-knock raids, and other things that violate the Fourth Amendment. If Democrats had consistently opposed these things, we probably wouldn't have them. But Democrats have consistently *supported* them.

And then there's war. When Republican George W. Bush decided he wanted to invade Iraq, a bunch of Democrats in Congress said, "Sure, we'll let him do that." Of course, those same Democrats blamed him later when things didn't go well—but the war might never have happened if Democrats had lined up to oppose it.

War hypocrisy doesn't just affect Democratic politicians, but also Democratic voters. When George W. Bush was president, Democrats attended war protests by the thousands. As soon as a Democrat, Barack Obama, was elected to replace him, the war protests stopped—even though the wars and occupations of Afghanistan and Iraq continued. (And of course, the Democrats in Congress stopped complaining.) I guess Democrats are only anti-war when a Republican is president. Libertarians, on the other hand, were outspoken opponents of the wars in Iraq and Afghanistan, regardless of who was president.

Basically the same thing is true of the Patriot Act, which has caused horrible violations of our civil liberties. Enough Democrats in Congress supported it to make sure it would pass. But then they attacked Republicans for it later. And Democratic voters used to protest the Patriot Act, but those protests stopped once Obama became president.

At the local level, Democrats ought to be diligent about preventing police brutality, and making sure the police respect everyone's rights. But actually, they don't care. They're generally happy to let the police do whatever they can get away with. Since the police usually treat minorities worse than whites, it's especially hypocritical.

I used to think the A.C.L.U. mostly fought against things supported by Republicans. Now I notice they are frequently fighting against policies supported by Democrats as well.

Democrats Bill and Hillary Clinton once supported the Defense of Marriage Act, which prohibited same-sex marriages. In 2013, Hillary changed her mind and started supporting the right of gays to get married. Libertarians have always supported getting government out of marriage, so people can marry whoever they want.

I think Libertarian pressure on issues like allowing gay marriage and ending the war on drugs has occasionally caused Democrats to stop being hypocrites and adopt Libertarian policies.

There was a brief period in 2009 when Democrats controlled the U.S. House, the presidency, *and* they had a filibuster-proof majority in the U.S. Senate. They could have rammed through anything they wanted to. They could have ended the Defense of Marriage Act, ended the Patriot Act, stopped the wars, passed tolerant immigration laws, or ended federal prohibition of drugs. They didn't do any of those things. If you ever doubt that Democrats are hypocrites, just remember that.

Unfortunately, there's still a general perception out there that Democrats are better than Republicans on these issues (civil liberties, foreign policy, and helping the poor and minority groups). They really aren't. They're just good at *pretending to care.*

CHAPTER 8

HOW MANY LIBERTARIANS ARE THERE?

Not enough! But we're working on it.

Actually, this question could mean several different things:

1. How many people have a libertarian point of view?
2. How many people are members of the Libertarian Party?
3. How many people regularly vote for Libertarian candidates?

Let's start with question 1: How many people have a libertarian point of view?

The number of libertarians depends on what you are counting and how you ask the question. According to a study released May 4, 2010 by Pew Research, "Reactions to the word 'libertarian' are evenly divided—38% positive, 37% negative. On balance, Republicans view 'libertarian' negatively, Democrats are divided, while independents have a positive impression of the term."

According to a study by the Cato Institute, a 2006 Zogby poll posed the following question to a sample of voters: "Would you describe yourself as fiscally conservative and socially liberal, also known as libertarian?" 44% of the respondents said "Yes." The Cato study goes on to say that about 15% of voters generally support libertarian principles.

Like I said, it depends on how you ask the question and what you're measuring. Different surveys come up with varying numbers, but I think it's fair to say about 15% of Americans have generally libertarian views, even if they don't call themselves "libertarian."

In a 2012 poll conducted by Pulse Opinion Research, 1,000 likely voters were asked the following: "In political terms, do you consider yourself conservative, moderate, liberal, or libertarian?" The responses were as follows: liberal 19%, moderate 37%, conservative 35%, libertarian 5%, not sure 4%. Now, this poll was actually commissioned by Libertarian Action Super PAC (LASPAC), which I founded. Can you believe it? I had to ask the question myself! There are many polls out there that give people the options "liberal, moderate, conservative," but we were having a really hard time finding polls that included "libertarian" as a label. So, while about 15% of the voters may support a libertarian philosophy, we found that only 5% call themselves libertarian.

In 2006, Gallup conducted a poll that allowed people to claim as many labels as they wanted: conservative, liberal, moderate, progressive, libertarian, and/or populist. When they did that, 10% of the people surveyed included "libertarian" as one of their labels.

Okay, now question 2: How many people are members of the Libertarian Party?

Even that isn't easy to answer. The Libertarian Party counts their membership in various ways. The numbers I'll report here are from the January 2013 Libertarian National Committee Membership Report. There were 14,029 "bylaws sustaining members" which basically means dues-paying members. That included 2,216 Lifetime Members which means, in most cases, they contributed $1,000 or more in a one-year period to the Libertarian Party.

Dues-paying membership peaked at about 33,000 back in the year 2000. I don't think that's because the number of libertarians was higher then, but instead because the Libertarian Party conducted a huge (and very expensive) recruitment drive.

However, technically you don't have to pay dues to be a member of the Libertarian Party. All you have to do is sign the membership pledge. According to that same membership report, 127,367 people were on record as having signed the membership pledge since the party's founding. That probably overstates the number who currently consider themselves members of the party—I think it would be misleading to say "The Libertarian Party has 127,000 members."

Some state and county Libertarian Party chapters have their own membership programs that are separate from the national party membership. I don't have statistics on how many additional dues-paying members that would be, but it wouldn't be very many, maybe an additional 1,000 or so.

There's also a totally different way to measure party membership. In 31 states, you can designate your political party when you register to vote. (Voter registration rules are different in each state, and they change from time to time.)

The Libertarian Party sometimes gets mistreated on voter registration forms. For example, in Kentucky they print the Republican and Democratic parties on the forms and you just have to check a box, but if you want to register as a Libertarian, then you have to check the "other" box and write the word "Libertarian." in the blank. In some states, they have occasionally deleted the Libertarian designation from the voter rolls and made the Libertarian Party start over from zero. I'm certain the percentage of registered Libertarians compared to Democrats and Republicans is lower than it would be if we had a level playing field.

The October 2012 issue of *Ballot Access News* listed 31 states allowing voter registration by party, with only 26 states reporting the number of registered Libertarians. There were a grand total of 325,807 registered Libertarians. That was 0.31% of all the registered voters, compared to 41.88% Democrats, 30.13% Republicans, 25.73% independents, 0.24% Greens, and 0.07% Constitution Party.

And now question 3: How many people regularly vote for Libertarian candidates?

Gary Johnson, the 2012 Libertarian nominee for President received around 1,275,000 votes, or 0.99% of the total, but he was only on the ballot in 48 states and D.C. (Michigan counted write-in votes for Johnson, but Oklahoma refused to allow write-ins.)

The presidential result is a bit misleading, because that's usually one of our worst percentages in the country! Libertarians get higher vote percentages in smaller races. The average for a Libertarian for U.S. Congress, when running against both a Republican and Democrat, is around 3%. In 2010, Libertarian Carlos Rodriguez received 8% for U.S. Congress District 28 in California. The top Libertarian percentage in 2010 for a state legislative office was 21% for Rex Bell, running for Indiana State House District 54. (Those were three-way races that included a Libertarian, a Democrat, and a Republican.)

Libertarians get much higher percentages when it's a two-way race, in other words Libertarian vs. Republican or Libertarian vs. Democrat.

Libertarians have won lots of nonpartisan local races, but wins in partisan elections are rare.

Some countries, particularly in Europe and South America, have legislatures with proportional representation. In a proportional representation system, if your party gets 5% of the vote, then your party gets around 5% of the seats in the legislature. It's much easier for third parties to win seats in countries like that. The U.S. has single-member winner-take-all "plurality" elections at the national level and in most states, which seems to lead toward a two-party system.

So, back to the original question, "How many Libertarians are there?" Here's my best answer: There are about 326,000 registered Libertarians, and about 14,000 dues-paying members of the Libertarian Party. Libertarians usually get around 3-5% of the vote in races against Republicans and Democrats. About 15% of voters generally support libertarian political views, and somewhere around 5-10% would call themselves libertarians.

CHAPTER 9

THE LIBERTARIAN PARTY PLATFORM

The Libertarian Party Platform is the official document describing the Libertarian Party's principles and positions on many issues. The original platform document was adopted in 1972, soon after the party was formed, and it gets amended at most Libertarian Party national conventions. (But the "Statement of Principles" has not changed for many years.)

As with most parties, Libertarians argue with each other about the platform. Should it be more radical, or less radical? Should it avoid controversial issues like abortion, war, and immigration? How detailed should it be?

Here's the most recent version of the platform, starting on the next page.

LIBERTARIAN PARTY PLATFORM

As adopted in Convention, May 2012, Las Vegas, Nevada

PREAMBLE

As Libertarians, we seek a world of liberty; a world in which all individuals are sovereign over their own lives and no one is forced to sacrifice his or her values for the benefit of others.

We believe that respect for individual rights is the essential precondition for a free and prosperous world, that force and fraud must be banished from human relationships, and that only through freedom can peace and prosperity be realized.

Consequently, we defend each person's right to engage in any activity that is peaceful and honest, and welcome the diversity that freedom brings. The world we seek to build is one where individuals are free to follow their own dreams in their own ways, without interference from government or any authoritarian power.

In the following pages we have set forth our basic principles and enumerated various policy stands derived from those principles.

These specific policies are not our goal, however. Our goal is nothing more nor less than a world set free in our lifetime, and it is to this end that we take these stands.

STATEMENT OF PRINCIPLES

We, the members of the Libertarian Party, challenge the cult of the omnipotent state and defend the rights of the individual.

We hold that all individuals have the right to exercise sole dominion over their own lives, and have the right to live in whatever manner they choose, so long as they do not forcibly interfere with the equal right of others to live in whatever manner they choose.

Governments throughout history have regularly operated on the opposite principle, that the State has the right to dispose of the lives of individuals and the fruits of their labor. Even within the United States, all political parties other than our own grant to government the right to regulate the lives of individuals and seize the fruits of their labor without their consent.

We, on the contrary, deny the right of any government to do these things, and hold that where governments exist, they must not violate the rights of any individual: namely, (1) the right to life—accordingly we support the prohibition of the initiation of physical force against others; (2) the right to liberty of speech and action—accordingly we oppose all attempts by government to abridge the freedom of speech and press, as well as government censorship in any form; and (3) the right to property—accordingly we oppose all government interference with private property, such as confiscation, nationalization, and eminent domain, and support the prohibition of robbery, trespass, fraud, and misrepresentation.

Since governments, when instituted, must not violate individual rights, we oppose all interference by government in the areas of voluntary and contractual relations among individuals. People should not be forced to sacrifice their lives and property for the benefit of others. They should be left free by government to deal with one another as free traders; and the resultant economic system, the only one compatible with the protection of individual rights, is the free market.

1.0 Personal Liberty

Individuals should be free to make choices for themselves and to accept responsibility for the consequences of the choices they make. No individual, group, or government may initiate force against any other individual, group, or government. Our support of an individual's right to make choices in life does not mean that we necessarily approve or disapprove of those choices.

1.1 Expression and Communication

We support full freedom of expression and oppose government censorship, regulation or control of communications media and technology. We favor the freedom to engage in or abstain from any religious activities that do not violate the rights of others. We oppose government actions which either aid or attack any religion.

1.2 Personal Privacy

Libertarians support the rights recognized by the Fourth Amendment to be secure in our persons, homes, and property. Protection from unreasonable search and seizure should include records held by third parties, such as email, medical, and library records. Only actions that infringe on the rights of others can properly be termed crimes. We favor the repeal of all laws creating "crimes" without victims, such as the use of drugs for medicinal or recreational purposes.

1.3 Personal Relationships

Sexual orientation, preference, gender, or gender identity should have no impact on the government's treatment of individuals, such as in current marriage, child custody, adoption, immigration or military service laws. Government does not have the authority to define, license or restrict personal relationships. Consenting adults should be free to choose their own sexual practices and personal relationships.

1.4 Abortion

Recognizing that abortion is a sensitive issue and that people can hold good-faith views on all sides, we believe that government should be kept out of the matter, leaving the question to each person for their conscientious consideration.

1.5 Crime and Justice

Government exists to protect the rights of every individual including life, liberty and property. Criminal laws should be limited to violation of the rights of others through force or fraud, or deliberate actions that place others involuntarily at significant risk of harm. Individuals retain the right to voluntarily assume risk of harm to themselves. We support restitution to the victim to the fullest degree possible at the expense of the criminal or the negligent wrongdoer. We oppose reduction of constitutional safeguards of the rights of the criminally accused. The rights of due process, a speedy trial, legal counsel, trial by jury, and the legal presumption of innocence until proven guilty, must not be denied. We assert the common-law right of juries to judge not only the facts but also the justice of the law.

1.6 Self-Defense

The only legitimate use of force is in defense of individual rights—life, liberty, and justly acquired property—against aggression. This right inheres in the individual, who may agree to be aided by any other individual or group. We affirm the individual right recognized by the Second Amendment to keep and bear arms, and oppose the prosecution of individuals for exercising their rights of self-defense. We oppose all laws at any level of government requiring registration of, or restricting, the ownership, manufacture, or transfer or sale of firearms or ammunition.

2.0 Economic Liberty

Libertarians want all members of society to have abundant opportunities to achieve economic success. A free and competitive market allocates resources in the most efficient manner. Each person has the right to offer goods and services to others on the free market. The only proper role of government in the economic realm is to protect property rights, adjudicate disputes, and provide a legal framework in which voluntary trade is protected. All efforts by government to redistribute wealth, or to control or manage trade, are improper in a free society.

2.1 Property and Contract

Property rights are entitled to the same protection as all other human rights. The owners of property have the full right to control, use, dispose of, or in any manner enjoy, their property without interference, until and unless the exercise of their control infringes the valid rights of others. We oppose all controls on wages, prices, rents, profits, production, and interest rates. We advocate the repeal of all laws banning or restricting the advertising of prices, products, or services. We oppose all violations of the right to private property, liberty of contract, and freedom of trade. The right to trade includes the right not to trade—for any reasons whatsoever. Where property, including land, has been taken from its rightful owners by the government or private action in violation of individual rights, we favor restitution to the rightful owners.

2.2 Environment

We support a clean and healthy environment and sensible use of our natural resources. Private landowners and conservation groups have a vested interest in maintaining natural resources. Pollution and misuse of resources cause damage to our ecosystem. Governments, unlike private businesses, are unaccountable for such damage done to our environment and have a terrible track record when it comes to environmental protection. Protecting the environment requires a clear definition and enforcement of individual rights in resources like land, water, air, and wildlife. Free markets and property rights stimulate the technological innovations and behavioral changes required to protect our environment and ecosystems. We realize that our planet's climate is constantly changing, but environmental advocates and social pressure are the most effective means of changing public behavior.

2.3 Energy and Resources

While energy is needed to fuel a modern society, government should not be subsidizing any particular form of energy. We oppose all government control of energy pricing, allocation, and production.

2.4 Government Finance and Spending

All persons are entitled to keep the fruits of their labor. We call for the repeal of the income tax, the abolishment of the Internal Revenue Service and all federal programs and services not required under the U.S. Constitution. We oppose any legal requirements forcing employers to serve as tax collectors. Government should not incur debt, which burdens future generations without their consent. We support the passage of a "Balanced Budget Amendment" to the

U.S. Constitution, provided that the budget is balanced exclusively by cutting expenditures, and not by raising taxes.

2.5 Money and Financial Markets

We favor free-market banking, with unrestricted competition among banks and depository institutions of all types. Individuals engaged in voluntary exchange should be free to use as money any mutually agreeable commodity or item. We support a halt to inflationary monetary policies and unconstitutional legal tender laws.

2.6 Monopolies and Corporations

We defend the right of individuals to form corporations, cooperatives and other types of companies based on voluntary association. We seek to divest government of all functions that can be provided by non-governmental organizations or private individuals. We oppose government subsidies to business, labor, or any other special interest. Industries should be governed by free markets.

2.7 Labor Markets

We support repeal of all laws which impede the ability of any person to find employment. We oppose government-fostered forced retirement. We support the right of free persons to associate or not associate in labor unions, and an employer should have the right to recognize or refuse to recognize a union. We oppose government interference in bargaining, such as compulsory arbitration or imposing an obligation to bargain.

2.8 Education

Education is best provided by the free market, achieving greater quality, accountability and efficiency with more diversity of choice. Recognizing that the education of children is a parental responsibility, we would restore authority to parents to determine the education of their children, without interference from government. Parents should have control of and responsibility for all funds expended for their children's education.

2.9 Health Care

We favor restoring and reviving a free market health care system. We recognize the freedom of individuals to determine the level of health insurance they want (if any), the level of health care they want, the care providers they want, the medicines and treatments they will use and all other aspects of their medical care, including end-of-life decisions. People should be free to purchase health insurance across state lines.

2.10 Retirement and Income Security

Retirement planning is the responsibility of the individual, not the government. Libertarians would phase out the current government-sponsored Social Security system and transition to a private voluntary system. The proper and most effective source of help for the poor is the voluntary efforts of private groups and individuals. We believe members of society will become more charitable and civil society will be strengthened as government reduces its activity in this realm.

3.0 Securing Liberty

The protection of individual rights is the only proper purpose of government. Government is constitutionally limited so as to prevent the infringement of individual rights by the government itself. The principle of non-initiation of force should guide the relationships between governments.

3.1 National Defense

We support the maintenance of a sufficient military to defend the United States against aggression. The United States should both avoid entangling alliances and abandon its attempts to act as policeman for the world. We oppose any form of compulsory national service.

3.2 Internal Security and Individual Rights

The defense of the country requires that we have adequate intelligence to detect and to counter threats to domestic security. This requirement must not take priority over maintaining the civil liberties of our citizens. The Constitution and Bill of Rights shall not be suspended even during time of war. Intelligence agencies that legitimately seek to preserve the security of the nation must be subject to oversight and transparency. We oppose the government's use of secret classifications to keep from the public information that it should have, especially that which shows that the government has violated the law.

3.3 International Affairs

American foreign policy should seek an America at peace with the world. Our foreign policy should emphasize defense against attack from abroad and enhance the likelihood of peace by avoiding foreign entanglements. We would end the current U.S. government policy of foreign intervention, including military and economic aid. We recognize the right of all people to resist tyranny and defend themselves and their rights. We condemn the use of force, and especially the use of terrorism, against the innocent, regardless of whether such acts are committed by governments or by political or revolutionary groups.

3.4 Free Trade and Migration

We support the removal of governmental impediments to free trade. Political freedom and escape from tyranny demand that individuals not be unreasonably constrained by government in the crossing of political boundaries. Economic freedom demands the unrestricted movement of human as well as financial capital across national borders. However, we support control over the entry into our country of foreign nationals who pose a credible threat to security, health or property.

3.5 Rights and Discrimination

Libertarians embrace the concept that all people are born with certain inherent rights. We reject the idea that a natural right can ever impose an obligation upon others to fulfill that "right." We condemn bigotry as irrational and repugnant. Government should neither deny nor abridge any individual's human right based upon sex, wealth, ethnicity, creed, age, national origin, personal habits, political preference or sexual orientation. Parents, or other guardians, have the right to raise their children according to their own standards and beliefs. This statement shall not be construed to condone child abuse or neglect.

3.6 Representative Government

We support election systems that are more representative of the electorate at the federal, state and local levels. As private voluntary groups, political parties should be allowed to establish their own rules for nomination procedures, primaries and conventions. We call for an end to any tax-financed subsidies to candidates or parties and the repeal of all laws which restrict voluntary financing of election campaigns. We oppose laws that effectively exclude alternative candidates and parties, deny ballot access, gerrymander districts, or deny the voters their right to consider all legitimate alternatives. We advocate initiative, referendum, recall and repeal when used as popular checks on government.

3.7 Self-Determination

Whenever any form of government becomes destructive of individual liberty, it is the right of the people to alter or to abolish it, and to agree to such new governance as to them shall seem most likely to protect their liberty.

4.0 Omissions

Our silence about any other particular government law, regulation, ordinance, directive, edict, control, regulatory agency, activity, or machination should not be construed to imply approval.

PART II
THE PRACTICAL SIDE

CHAPTER 10

THE WORLD'S SMALLEST POLITICAL QUIZ

If you've been to college, you may remember how during the first week of the semester, all the clubs and organizations set up tables and booths and try to recruit new members and get people involved.

Well, it was my first week in the MBA program at the University of Michigan, and I was walking through the quadrangle past all of the clubs and organizations.

One guy asked me as I walked by, "Do you want to take the World's Smallest Political Quiz?"

Since I had spent countless hours over the previous decade debating politics, and seeing that this person probably wanted to provoke a political debate, I wasn't going to miss the opportunity. So I took The Quiz!

The World's Smallest Political Quiz has ten questions and it tells you whether you are liberal, conservative, libertarian, authoritarian, or centrist. It's printed on the next page.

Libertarians often refer to it as "The Quiz." The Quiz is also on the cover of this book, and it's easy to find all over the Internet by searching for "World's Smallest Political Quiz."

World's Smallest Political Quiz

WHERE DO YOU STAND POLITICALLY? To find out, take the world-famous World's Smallest Political Quiz. For each statement, circle A for Agree, M for Maybe, or D for Disagree.

How do you stand on PERSONAL issues? 20 10 0

- Government should not censor speech, press, media or Internet. A M D
- Military service should be voluntary. There should be no draft. A M D
- There should be no laws regarding sex between consenting adults A M D
- Repeal laws prohibiting adult possession and use of drugs. A M D
- There should be no National ID card A M D

SCORING 20 for every A, 10 for every M, and 0 for every D: _____

How do you stand on ECONOMIC issues? 20 10 0

- End "corporate welfare." No government handouts to business. A M D
- End government barriers to international free trade. A M D
- Let people control their own retirement: privatize Social Security. A M D
- Replace government welfare with private charity. A M D
- Cut taxes and government spending by 50% or more. A M D

SCORING 20 for every A, 10 for every M, and 0 for every D: _____

NOW FIND YOUR PLACE ON THE CHART!

Mark your **PERSONAL** score on the lower-left scale; your **ECONOMIC** score on the lower-right. Then follow the grid lines until they meet at your political position. The Chart shows the political group that agrees with you most. Liberals tend to value personal freedom. Conservatives tend to value economic freedom. Libertarians value both. Statists are against both.

To learn more about this Quiz, see other side.

"The World's Smallest Political Quiz is **savvy** and willing to tell you the **truth**."
—*YAHOO! MAGAZINE*

LIBERTARIAN

LEFT (Liberal) · CENTRIST · RIGHT (Conservative)

STATIST (Big Government)

PERSONAL ISSUES SCORE · ECONOMIC ISSUES SCORE

Chart adapted from an original idea by David Nolan
© The Advocates for Self-Government

OK TO REPRINT QUIZ WITHOUT MODIFICATIONS WITH CREDIT TO THE ADVOCATES

The Quiz tries to break the paradigm that politics is a linear spectrum from left to right. (You're either liberal, conservative, or in between.) Instead, The Quiz plots political views on a two-dimensional graph with personal issues on one axis, and economic issues on the other. It helps make the point that libertarianism is a separate thing from liberalism and conservatism.

If you haven't ever taken The Quiz, take it now! What was your score? What sector did you end up in?

Unfortunately, I can't remember my exact score the first time I took The Quiz. But I think I scored 90 on the personal issues, and 100 on the economic issues. That means I was almost a total libertarian!

So, which item did I fail to score libertarian on? I can't remember for sure, but I think it had to do with immigration. The questions on the older version of The Quiz that I took were slightly different than the ones I quoted above. The older version of The Quiz included the statement, "Let peaceful people immigrate or emigrate freely." At the time, that didn't sound quite right to me.

I was not born a libertarian, and I had barely heard of the word "libertarian" before I took The Quiz. But shortly after I took it and found out I had libertarian political views, I joined the Libertarian Party as a dues-paying member. I was excited to have finally found a group of people that felt the same way I did. In 1997 I signed up for a $30-per-month pledge to the Libertarian Party, even though I had to pay for it out of savings since I was a full-time graduate student.

I had started changing my views on some issues before I became a Libertarian. After I joined the Libertarian Party, my political views continued to evolve in a libertarian direction. That was partly because I was exposed to many well-written libertarian arguments for the first time. I truly changed my position on some major issues, like immigration. Many libertarians have pointed out that the more time you spend thinking about the libertarian point of view, the more appealing it becomes.

I'm not the only person who joined the Libertarian Party after taking The Quiz. I actually think The Quiz is the Libertarian Party's most valuable and effective outreach tool. Setting up a Quiz booth and giving The Quiz to as many people as possible is a great project for a new Libertarian Party activist. The Advocates for Self-Government offers cheap copies of The Quiz in many forms: posters, small paper copies, and multiple sizes of cards.

I want to offer a big thanks to the Advocates for Self-Government for creating the World's Smallest Political Quiz, and to James Hudler, the Michigan Libertarian who was manning the booth and offered me The Quiz that day I walked through the quadrangle.

CHAPTER 11

HISTORY OF THE LIBERTARIAN PARTY

The Libertarian Party was founded on December 11, 1971 in Colorado Springs, Colorado. The founders were a group of eight activists including the late David F. Nolan, whom many view as the father of the Libertarian Party.

An M.I.T. political science graduate, Mr. Nolan had reservations about working within the Democratic or Republican Party, and he was working to build a new coalition he called "the libertarian movement."

In January 1971, Nolan wrote an article for *The Individualist* magazine in which he presented the two-dimensional diamond-shaped chart that became known as the Nolan Chart. The chart categorized political action into two categories, economic and personal, and later was adapted to become part of the World's Smallest Political Quiz.

Later in 1971, Nolan wrote another article for *The Individualist*, called "The Case for A Libertarian Political Party." In that article, he gave six reasons libertarians should form their own political party:

First, and perhaps most important, we will be able to get a great deal more news coverage for ourselves and our ideas than we have ever gotten before. Public interest in political issues and philosophies is always at an all-time high during Presidential election years, and the media people are actively seeking news in this area.

As a direct consequence of this fact, we will probably reach (and hopefully convert) far more people than we usually do; hopefully, some of these people will turn out to support our candidates, and will thus enable to locate hitherto-unlocatable libertarians (or at least sympathizers).

Third, we will be able to get some idea of how much support we really do have (at least in potential form) around the country; if we can get 100,000 votes the first time out, we know there are at least 100,000 libertarians out there—and whatever number we get, we can figure that it represents only a small fraction of the total, as not all of our potential supporters will even hear about our efforts, and many of those who do will be in States where we can't get on the ballot.

Fourth, a libertarian political party would provide a continuing "focal point" for libertarian activity—something that "one-shot" projects do not provide.

Fifth, we will be able to hasten the already emerging coalition between the libertarian "left" and libertarian "right". At the moment, the former group is supporting people like Eugene McCarthy, while the latter is supporting people like Barry Goldwater. A truly libertarian party would draw support both from such "leftist" groups as the Institute for the Study of Non-Violence and the American Civil Liberties Union, and from "rightist" groups like the John Birch Society and the Liberty Amendment Committee, however. This would increase the political impact of the libertarian "movement", as "leftist" and "rightist" libertarians now usually wind up voting so as to cancel each other (when they vote at all). Furthermore, libertarian votes now get lumped in with "liberal" and "conservative" votes, whereas the votes received by a libertarian party would not be hidden in this manner.

A sixth point in favor of establishing a libertarian party is that by its mere existence, it would put some pressure on the other parties to take a more libertarian stand.

An finally, there is always the possibility that we might actually get some libertarians elected.

Mr. Nolan and others had been increasingly concerned about civil liberties violations and the ongoing Vietnam War, as well as increasing burdens on economic freedom. In August 1971, President Richard Nixon appeared on television and announced he was taking the dollar off the gold standard and imposing wage and price controls. That announcement was the last straw that finally caused Mr. Nolan and others to officially form the Libertarian Party.

John Hospers, a philosophy professor at the University of Southern California, was nominated as the Libertarian Party's first presidential candidate in 1972. Tonie Nathan (a woman) was nominated for vice president. The ticket appeared on the ballot in only two states, but Hospers and Nathan each received one electoral vote. The 1976 Roger MacBride-David Bergland ticket made the ballot in 32 states and received over 170,000 votes.

Since then, the Libertarian Party has continued to field a presidential ticket in every election, three times appearing on the ballot in all fifty states. In 1980, Libertarian nominee Ed Clark got over 920,000 votes, which held the record for Libertarians for many years.

Ron Paul, who had left Congress in 1985, ran for president as the Libertarian nominee in 1988.

In 2012, former New Mexico Governor Gary Johnson ran as the Libertarian presidential nominee and received over 1,270,000 votes (about one percent of the nationwide vote), breaking Ed Clark's record.

When Libertarian presidential candidates keep receiving about one percent or less, it's fair to ask "why bother?" 1996 and 2000 Libertarian presidential nominee Harry Browne helped answer that question when he wrote after his 2000 campaign:

> Are LP presidential campaigns irrelevant? I don't think so. During 2000, I appeared on 53 national television shows and 90

national radio shows—plus 80 local TV shows and 375 local radio shows. I had hundreds of press and Internet interviews, and I gave dozens and dozens of speeches.

Browne went on to explain that many people hear about the Libertarian Party for the first time through the presidential campaign.

As a new Libertarian in 1996, I can personally attest that I felt more confident telling people I was a Libertarian after I saw Harry Browne's professionalism and communication skills. I remember feeling disappointed that he ended up getting so few votes, especially in 2000. But his explanation for why it's important to continue fielding Libertarian presidential candidates made sense to me. In some states with little local activity, the presidential candidate may be the only Libertarian on the ballot. Without the presidential campaign, volunteers and voters in those areas would have little to focus on. And the presidential campaign usually inspires lots of people to join the Libertarian Party.

Over the last 40 years, the Libertarian Party has run thousands of candidates for various offices around the United States. And sometimes Libertarians actually win elections. Most of the victories are in small towns, or involve Libertarians running in nonpartisan races (i.e., where no party label appears on the ballot).

In 1987, Libertarians won every seat on the council of the small town of Big Water, Utah. In 1994, more than 40 Libertarians were serving as elected or appointed public officials. In 2013, the Libertarian Party listed 136 Libertarians serving in elected office: 100 in nonpartisan offices, and 36 in partisan offices.

Since the Libertarian Party was formed, twelve Libertarians have been elected to the state legislatures of Alaska, New Hampshire and Vermont. (*LP News*, Vol. 41, Issue 2, page 9.) However, no Libertarian has ever won a race for Congress or any statewide office. Mike Fellows of Montana holds the record for a Libertarian in a statewide race, getting 43 percent in his campaign for clerk of the Montana Supreme Court in 2012. (LP.org blog, January 22, 2013.)

From the eight original members who founded the Libertarian Party in 1971, the number of dues-paying members has grown off and on, peaking in the year 2000 at just over 30,000. Then membership declined for a while. From 2006 to 2012, the number of dues-paying members hovered around 14,000-15,000.

David Nolan stayed active with the party throughout most of its history. (He died unexpectedly on November 21, 2010, in Tucson, Arizona, at the age of 66.) While I had admired Mr. Nolan for years, in 2010 I finally had the pleasure of working with him directly. I was then serving as the national executive director of the Libertarian Party in Washington, D.C., while Mr. Nolan had recently been elected to another term on the party's governing board, the Libertarian National Committee. Mr. Nolan was an enthusiastic and principled activist doing hard work right alongside newer members.

For a more complete history of the Libertarian Party and the libertarian movement in general, I recommend the 741-page book *Radicals for Capitalism: A Freewheeling History of the Modern American Libertarian Movement* by Brian Doherty. The book covers some of the 20th-century thinkers such as Ayn Rand, Nobel Prize-winning economist Milton Friedman, and many others, who laid the philosophical foundation upon which the Libertarian Party was built (though neither Rand nor Friedman joined the Libertarian Party). It's more than just a history book—sometimes hilarious, other times depressing, in many ways Doherty's book seems more like reality TV or a scandal rag as it chronicles the infighting, turf battles, and occasional romances gone bad.

However, the best source for extensive information on Libertarian Party history is the Internet, where you can find links to some decades-old copies of the national party's printed newsletter *LP News*, as well as newsletters from state and local affiliates and past

Libertarian Party candidates.

CHAPTER 12

HOW THE LIBERTARIAN PARTY IS ORGANIZED

The Libertarian Party has a national-level organization, along with state affiliates. These are all technically separate organizations. This chapter is focused on the national organization.

The "board of directors" of the Libertarian Party is called the Libertarian National Committee (LNC). The LNC is composed of around 27 members including the four officers (Chair, Vice-chair, Secretary, Treasurer), five at-large committee representatives, and around nine regional representatives plus nine regional alternates.

The LNC is elected at the biennial national conventions, which are made up of delegates sent by the state chapters. The national conventions are typically three- to five-day affairs involving long (and some would say tedious) business meetings, but also plenty of motivational speakers, presentations on current events, training sessions, and lots of socializing with fellow Libertarians.

The Libertarian Party used to have a reputation for national conventions involving a lot of marijuana and other drug use, but in recent times they've been more tame. Libertarian conventions are now probably no wilder than a typical engineers' or teachers' convention.

Attendance varies. At the 2006 national convention in Portland, Oregon, there were about 300 attendees. Around 800 people came to the 2012 national convention in Las Vegas. Attendance is usually better in presidential election years.

Delegates to the national convention elect the new LNC members, vote on proposals to modify the party platform and bylaws, and every four years they select the presidential and vice-presidential nominees.

Libertarian convention delegates are notorious for fighting over the platform—especially how radical or moderate it should be. People plot and strategize for more than a year before each convention. The platform is several pages long, and I bet some people spend more time working to change the platform than I spent writing this book! I think some people put a little too much energy into it. But that's okay—actually, all political party insiders fight about their platforms. Same goes for the bylaws.

In order to attend a national convention as a voting delegate, you have to be selected by your state party affiliate. Each state is allocated a certain number of delegates, based on a couple of factors indicating the strength of the Libertarian Party in that state.

Ultimately, the Libertarian Party is made up of its members. Many people first seek out the Libertarian Party at the national website, LP.org, and some join as dues-paying members for $25 or more. If you're interested, you can join online, or mail in a membership form, or call the toll-free number 1-800-ELECT-US. You can actually be a "card-carrying Libertarian": members get a membership card and also receive the printed newsletter, *LP News*.

A person can join with or without paying dues by signing a membership pledge based on the non-aggression principle. The pledge states, "I certify that I oppose the initiation of force to achieve political or social goals."

That pledge has caught some people's attention, so I want to pass along some information about it. In a September 2007 email talking about the background of the pledge, LP co-founder David Nolan wrote:

> I know what really motivated it, and why its specific wording was chosen. I know this because I wrote it all by myself (no committees!) and the reasoning I used was mine alone. The purpose of even having a pledge of this sort was in fact to differentiate the nascent LP from the radical-left groups of the 1960s. Back in 1971, there the Feds were actively infiltrating and sabotaging antiwar groups, and I wanted to send as signal that while we libertarians were calling for radical change, we were committed to using peaceful means. The specific wording, however, was intentionally "Randian" in tone, for as Tom [Knapp] notes, fans and followers of Ayn Rand made up the largest segment of the emerging libertarian movement at that time. Over time, a great deal of mythology has built up around this one simple sentence. Some people believe it was intended as the ultimate one-sentence definition of libertarian philosophy; others have interpreted it to mean that no form of government can be legitimate. These are interesting interpretations, to be sure, but they are only interpretations.

Whether or not they officially join the Libertarian Party, many people subscribe to the party's email announcements, which include press releases on current issues. Others join Libertarian Party-related social networks online.

The Libertarian Party has maintained a national headquarters in Washington, D.C. for most of its existence. In 1995, the party headquarters moved into the (infamous) Watergate Office Complex. As of 2013, the LNC was considering moving the headquarters to lower-priced space nearby in Virginia.

LP headquarters consists of paid staff led by an executive director. Over the past couple of decades the staff count has fluctuated from just a few to more than a dozen full-time employees, depending on what the budget can handle. The staff does a variety of things like answer phone calls, send fundraising letters and emails, maintain membership records, issue press releases and statements giving the Libertarian Party position on current issues, maintain the LP.org website, help to recruit and assist candidates nationwide, provide assistance to the state and local affiliates, and help plan the national conventions. The headquarters staff reports to the Chair of the LNC.

I served as the executive director myself from July 2009 through December 2011. For better or worse, there has been a lot of turnover in that position over the years. I think I did a pretty good job. In my exit notice, I pointed out the following four accomplishments:

1. The Libertarian Party has presented a libertarian message, differentiating us from conservatives and liberals.

2. Monthly pledge recurring revenue increased from $20,854 to $33,092.

3. The cash reserve or "money in the bank" has been at record levels.

4. Over 800 LP candidates ran in the November 2010 elections, up from around 600 in 2006 and 2008.

I also had to confess that the number of current donors had dropped from 14,977 to 13,981 during my tenure.

So that's basically how the national party is organized. I also want to mention a little bit about the state parties.

State parties have their own organizations with structures that are usually similar to the national party, with officers and other representatives on a state committee. The organizational structure varies from state to state, partly due to the election laws of different states. Some state affiliates have a dues requirement, and that may or may not affect a person's ability to vote at state conventions.

In many states, when you register to vote, you don't register with a particular party. However, in 31 states, you can select a party when you register. In December 2012, *Ballot Access News* reported there were 325,807 registered Libertarians in the U.S. In some cases, being registered as a Libertarian affects how you can participate with your state party.

Most state parties also have county chapters. Many new national LP members decide they want to be more active, so they look up their local county party and contact them about meetings and other events.

Almost all activists in the Libertarian Party are volunteers. At the time of writing this book, I'd guess there are about twenty paid Libertarian Party staffers throughout America, including the national headquarters staff.

CHAPTER 13

HOW I WON MY FIRST COUNTY CHAIRMAN POSITION!

I joined the Libertarian Party in 1996, but at first I didn't do much besides donate money and receive newsletters. I remember getting the first few issues of *LP News*, the national Libertarian Party's newsletter, and thinking with a bit of relief, "Wow! This doesn't suck!" I was glad that my small new political party could produce something reasonably professional.

After graduating from the University of Michigan with an MBA in 1998, I moved to Georgia to start a management consulting job. Once I was there, I decided it was time to do more than just donate money and read the Libertarian Party newsletters. I was ready to take action and volunteer.

I found a notice for monthly meetings of the Cobb County Libertarians, so that seemed like a good place to start. I was a bit disappointed when I showed up and found only two people there. I was even more disappointed when they told me they had been the only two people coming most of the time for the past five years!

It didn't seem like they wanted to do much. After a couple of meetings listening to them ramble, I became very impatient. I finally exclaimed something along the lines of, "Sitting here talking to each other is just a waste of time! We need to do something! Go door-to-door or something!"

Now, I considered myself to be a successful and talented person. I had done well in my first job as an engineer. I had a new MBA from the number two program in the nation (according to Business Week magazine). I was motivated. I was not about to let two surly old men get in the way of success!

Over the following weeks, I created my own brochure that I could print at home, called "Libertarian Short & Simple." It had a summary of the Libertarian Party's positions, where to get more information, and a membership form so people could join. It was very efficient!

I put hundreds of them up at apartments and even distributed some door-to-door in neighborhoods. I later called the party headquarters, eager to find out how many new members had joined the party using my brochure.

Much to my surprise, not a single person had joined as a result of my work.

A bit humbled, I started taking more guidance from the two men who had been there in the Libertarian Party trenches for years. They suggested having outreach booths at the county fair and gun shows where we could give people the World's Smallest Political Quiz and hand out literature about the Libertarian Party. Since I had found out about the party through a similar booth in Michigan, their suggestion made sense to me. I thought it was a bit of a slow approach, but I decided to try it their way.

By working at several outreach booths, I got experience speaking to voters in public, and I watched the experienced guys answering tough questions about the Libertarian Party.

At one point I found we had access to the Libertarian Party membership list for our county. I volunteered to start making phone calls to invite people to our monthly meetings, and I started sending email reminders too. Turnout at our meetings steadily grew. Then the original two men asked me to serve as the county chair, and I accepted. During the year and a half I lived in Georgia, average attendance at our meetings grew from three to about fifteen.

The point is, when I overcame my impatience and adopted more of a "slow and steady" approach, things worked better, and we made progress.

I grew to appreciate those two men who took me under their wings and helped an impatient know-it-all become a more effective activist. Their names are Nelson Barnhouse and Garret Michael Hayes and they continued to be active with the party. In fact Mr. Hayes was the 2002 and 2006 Libertarian nominee for governor of Georgia!

There were several times in the beginning when I felt like saying "To hell with the Libertarian Party—no one is doing anything! This is a waste of time!" There were times I was tempted to lash out rudely at Mr. Barnhouse and Mr. Hayes. Looking back, I'm glad I didn't cross the line from being impatient to becoming a complete jerk and a quitter.

Unfortunately, in the years since then, I've seen similar things happen to other new activists. They expect a well-oiled machine where everyone is working hard on a bunch of different tasks, and they find something much less impressive. Then they get impatient and demand that everyone work a lot harder—and when that doesn't happen, they get mad and quit.

I think it's more effective to be patient, steady, and show goodwill toward other Libertarian activists, even when they seem lazy, boring or arrogant.

I called this chapter "How I won my first county chairman position!" That made it sound exciting, right? In reality, it should probably be called "How I did a job no one else wanted to do." I look forward to the day when we have competitive elections throughout America to decide who gets to serve as the local Libertarian Party county chairs. I'd love to see people working their tails off throughout the year recruiting members, helping candidates, raising money, and then running against each other for county chair based on their track records of successful activism.

But the reality is, in most counties in America, we have vacancies in the Libertarian county chair position (and secretary and treasurer, etc.). Where we have organized county chapters, often the person serving as chair is the only person willing to do it. I am grateful to the dedicated men and women who step up and serve as county officers. It's not always easy serving as a county chair. It's not easy helping people find ways to be productive. It's not easy getting people to show up to meetings more than once. And in many cases, it's not easy keeping people focused on progress when they really seem to just want to fight with each other.

And you don't even get paid. Instead, you often end up paying for things like supplies and promotional items out of your own pocket.

But think of it this way: there are many, many opportunities for progress. It's actually not difficult to be a county chair, as long as you have what I'd call a "good attitude." If you're willing to be patient and watch things change gradually, and if you're willing to work with people's idiosyncrasies, it can be fun and rewarding. If you want to see a whole lot of stuff change overnight, then it's probably not the job for you.

If you are thinking about getting involved with the Libertarian Party, I recommend checking to see if there is a local county affiliate with meetings you can attend. If so, please be nice and try to find ways to help that don't pile more work on the current officers. And if there's no local affiliate, contact your state party to see about starting one up!

CHAPTER 14

TURNING AROUND THE DYSFUNCTIONAL TEXAS LIBERTARIAN PARTY

I moved to Austin, Texas in 2000 after becoming a joint owner of a small business there, and I soon got involved with the Travis County Libertarian Party. This is a story about what happened a few years after that. It's going to sound like I'm bragging a lot—I'm just warning you.

On October 30, 2003, I emailed all 59 county chairs and state committee members listed on the Libertarian Party of Texas website. I explained that the Libertarian Party of Texas had not qualified to put candidates on the ballot in 2004, so we would have to conduct a big petition drive. We needed to collect 45,540 "valid" petition signatures to re-qualify (in reality we'd have to collect a lot more), so I was asking people to step up as local volunteer coordinators and tell me how many signatures they thought their county could collect.

Much to my surprise, AOL froze my email account! What was going on? Was this some kind of conspiracy against Libertarians?

I had to phone AOL tech support to get the account re-activated. It turned out, they had frozen my account because nearly half of those emails had bounced.

Not to be defeated, I picked up the phone and started calling the county chairs at the phone numbers on the website. I discovered that many of the numbers were either disconnected, gave fax tones, or rang continuously without any answering system.

I began to fully realize the mess our state party organization had become. For the first time in eighteen years we faced a petition drive for ballot access, and our state and county organizations were in shambles. The state database manager had resigned, and our website was filled with outdated contact information.

A few months later, the state treasurer ceased activities. The state secretary hadn't published minutes for months. All of the officers had been fighting with each other, but then they stopped and basically went AWOL. While many of those individuals had been fine county activists, the group dynamics at the state level proved dysfunctional.

Fortunately, the Travis County chair, Pat Dixon, stepped into the void and agreed to head up a state ballot access committee to take charge of the petition drive. I agreed to serve as the statewide volunteer coordinator. Before then, I had only been a Travis County volunteer.

For six months I worked nearly full-time as an unpaid volunteer for the petition drive. I traveled the state training other petitioners, and I paid my own travel and hotel expenses without getting reimbursed. (I had recently sold the business in Austin, so I had the time and money to do this.) I thought that if I failed to step up at this crucial time when I was available and capable, how could I ever fault others for failing to step up?

Thanks to my efforts, and the efforts of some other very dedicated folks, the Texas LP turned in over 80,000 signatures in May 2004. Far more than 45,540 of those were valid, so we qualified for the ballot.

With momentum from the petition drive, Pat Dixon sought and won the state chairmanship of the Texas LP at the June 2004 state convention. I was hired to fill the newly created position of executive director—a position that came with a small paycheck. Before then, the party had been run completely by volunteers.

Shortly after taking my position as executive director, I proceeded to work with our new secretary to update our website contacts. On July 1, 2004, I phoned the 800 number listed on our website and left a voicemail to see what would happen. The outgoing message at the 800 number mentioned a candidate for governor from 2002, as well as another contact phone number. I dialed it—it was disconnected!

When I logged into the voicemail system for the 800 number, I found there were six months' worth of unchecked messages, and there had probably been more that got automatically deleted. Perhaps it had been *two years* since the voicemail had been checked. Here is a sample of transcripts of those voicemails:

"This is Michael at 210-###-####. Want to know if y'all have a twenty-eighth congressional district candidate. I would run as a Libertarian."

"Ross, interested in helping LP with campaigning in El Paso."

"Ken in Dallas. I called R. and the phone is disconnected. Chris's message center doesn't give anything to leave a message on. I'm in Arlington and want to get a hold of where the Gary Nolan campaign meeting will be. Maybe I'll get on the computer one day."

"Albert Wood with Valley Morning Star. We're doing a series of stories . . ."

"Hi, my name is Melvin. I'm trying to find a petition to sign."

"Hi, this is Wes Benedict, I was calling about the...the—

uh...this phone number...the uh 800-422-1776. I'm curious who gets these messages. If you'd give me a call. Thanks a lot and I hope this voicemail works. Thanks, bye."

In August and September 2004, I was bombarded by requests for contact information for our candidates. Unfortunately, much of that contact information was missing or incorrect. The press was begging for phone numbers and photos of our candidates, but I only had the information for some of them.

This description obviously sounds demoralizing—but actually, I was encouraged. There was nowhere to go but up! Libertarians often compain about our lack of press coverage, but I was finding that the press was begging to cover us if we would only let them! Volunteers were contacting us begging to help if we would only give them something to do! We were making it extremely difficult for voters to find out about our candidates, yet many voters still voted Libertarian that year.

Libertarian activists, libertarian couch potatoes and even non-libertarian press analysts often debate why the Libertarian Party hasn't achieved more success. Many say our platform is too radical, or if we would just drop this or that controversial issue, we'd have massive growth.

I wasn't sure how much our platform had to do with our success or failure, but I was confident that unanswered phones, outdated websites, and bad contact information were hurting us.

The good news, I thought, was that a Texas turnaround would be straightforward, with potential for major improvement. All I had to do was focus on the basics like customer service and cleaning up our websites, and things would surely improve.

Making improvements was tough at first. At one point I sent a batch of fundraising letters, and then I found out that our treasurer was too busy with his personal life to retrieve the funds and deposit them in the bank!

Eventually another volunteer stepped in to serve as treasurer, Geoffrey Neale. Among many other roles, Neale had previously served as national chair, but thankfully he was willing to serve where we critically needed him. He set up an accounting system and kept the funds moving to the bank account.

I wanted to hire an assistant director to help with database management, writing, and anything else I could delegate. I wanted to get fellow Travis County activist Arthur DiBianca, who had been a valuable volunteer on the ballot access campaign. I sent a note to our state committee saying, "Art has proven to be one of those super productive workers capable of producing up to ten times the output of the average citizen" (which was true). The committee approved. Finally, I felt we had a team that could make big things happen.

We set out with a goal to recruit a record number of candidates for 2006. The previous record had been 138 in Texas. We succeeded and got 168 Libertarians on the ballot in 2006. In fact, we broke lots of records in 2006 (and again in 2008), making Texas the best performing Libertarian state chapter by most measures. We did this against a trend of declining performance of the LP nationwide. We recruited a record 173 LP candidates in Texas for the November 2008 elections, which was 29% of the nationwide Libertarian total. Even though Texas has just 8% of the U.S. population, Texas LP candidates in 2008 received 28% of all the Libertarian votes for U.S. House and 44% of all the Libertarian votes for State Representative. Our list of Texas Libertarians elected to nonpartisan offices grew from two to eight. We increased the Texas LP donor base from under 300 in 2005 to over 900 in 2008. We wrote highly successful fundraising letters and emails. We raised $244,000 for the 2007-2008 election cycle, which was more than the state parties of California, Florida and New York combined.

There was no magic bullet to what we did. We didn't do anything especially exciting or new. We just focused on the basics and copied the strategies and techniques used by earlier successful Libertarian Party efforts. Much of the work boiled down to taking care of lots of details.

While I enjoyed working as executive director in Texas, I was paid very little. I gave several months' notice that I would leave at the end of 2008 to get a "real job" and rebuild my personal bank accounts.

A part of me hoped the Texas LP would come crashing down after I left, just to make it clear to everyone that I was responsible for the success. However, there were hundreds and hundreds of volunteers and donors that supported our efforts, and I don't think they did it just to make me look good. So, I helped recruit and train my replacement, Robert Butler. His fundraising beat my records, and his candidate recruitment was quite strong.

Okay, so why have I told you all this? Because I know that other Libertarians have had a similar experience of thinking their local or state organization is a total wreck. I want to make the point that a dysfunctional and declining Libertarian state party can be turned around pretty quickly, and it can come roaring back to break records. Currently, many Libertarian state party organizations are weak. In 2012, only sixteen states had ten or more candidates. I'd like to see every state field a hundred Libertarian candidates.

Unfortunately, party committees can sometimes act as obstacles. In Chapter 22, I'll suggest how to get around internal barriers to success by forming political action committees.

CHAPTER 15

WHY RUN FOR OFFICE AS A LIBERTARIAN?

Obviously, when Libertarians get elected, they can implement libertarian principles directly.

But Libertarians don't win very often, so what's the point of running?

Here's how I see it. As a Libertarian activist, you've got options. You can spend your weekends at tax protests or civil liberties protests, or pro-liberty conferences, and be one more voice making the freedom movement just a bit louder.

Or, you can run for office as a Libertarian and amplify your voice a thousand times.

Libertarian candidates, whether or not they win, get tens of thousands of dollars' worth of free publicity. Instead of just sitting on the couch shouting at your Congressperson on television, if you run for Congress as a Libertarian, there's actually a decent chance you'll get to shout directly to her face on live television in front of tens of thousands of viewers!

Libertarians don't always get invited to debates, but lots of times we do! In 2008, just after the TARP bank bailouts were passed, the

Texas Libertarian candidate for U.S. Senate, Yvonne Schick, was invited to a televised debate. Schick was able to tell incumbent Republican Senator John Cornyn on live statewide television that his votes for the bailouts were wrong.

The co-founder of the Libertarian Party, David Nolan, ran for U.S. Senate in 2010 against incumbent John McCain in Arizona. While Nolan didn't win, he received 4.7%. He also got to debate Senator McCain on television and was able to point out how John McCain had voted for things like the Patriot Act, which threatened our civil liberties.

It would cost tens of thousands of dollars to pay for pro-Libertarian ads that get as much publicity as what you can get for free when you run for office. And it doesn't just stop with televised debates. Libertarian candidates are often included in newspaper stories, invited as guests on talk radio, and are included in widely distributed publications like the League of Women Voters Guide.

Running for office as a Libertarian can be like making a $10,000 or even a $50,000 contribution to the Libertarian Party!

Unfortunately, the Republicans and Democrats have created rules that prohibit Libertarians from participating in some events. For example, they won't allow the Libertarian candidate for president up on stage to debate the Republican and Democrat. (After independent Ross Perot got 18% in 1992, they put a stop to that kind of competition.) But Libertarians still get included in lots of events at the state and local levels.

I have recruited hundreds of candidates and have run for office five times myself. Nothing does more to turn a couch potato into a super activist than putting him or her on the ballot for some office—any office. Libertarian candidates get their friends and family to help them—people who never would have gotten involved with the Libertarian Party otherwise.

The first time I ran for office was for Travis County

Commissioner in Texas in 2002. I was scared to death of public speaking, but I decided to run anyway to be part of the team of Libertarian candidates.

When I say scared of public speaking, I mean that in college it was so bad that when I gave a report I would shake, sweat, I could hardly breathe, and it was painfully obvious to the rest of the class. I got a little better after making a bunch of presentations at work, but speaking to a political crowd was still frightening to me.

At one of my first appearances, I did so poorly that my stomach hurt for two days after the event. It wasn't just my imagination. I had a video tape to re-live the horror (which I've since destroyed). I was completely embarrassed and disgusted with myself. Maybe I wasn't going to completly drop out of the race, but I was about ready to quit any campaigning. But I went to one more event, and that went a little better. Each time I did something, I felt a little more comfortable. In the end, I received 5% of the vote against a Republican and Democrat. Not much, but I had gotten some exposure and experience, and I felt more comfortable.

A year later I had sold my business and decided to run for Austin City Council. It was a nonpartisan election, so the word "Libertarian" was not by my name on the ballot. But the press routinely reported the fact that I was a Libertarian. And I was invited to about 40 public events! The beauty of running for office is that you don't have to organize these events yourself. Neighborhood associations, environmental groups, various Democrat and Republican clubs, news organizations and many others will organize events for all the candidates and invite you to participate.

In that city council race, not only did I attend the public events, but I organized 37 volunteers to distribute over 12,000 campaign flyers door-to-door, and I had several volunteers make phone calls to promote my campaign. I didn't win, but I ended up receiving 35% of the vote in a city-wide election. None of that activity would have happened if I hadn't run for office. That's the power of running for office—the activity and publicity it generates.

I truly believe that, win or lose, every vote for a Libertarian makes a difference. And the more Libertarians on the ballot, the bigger the difference. Besides the activity and publicity, Libertarian candidates put pressure on Democrats and Republicans to move in a Libertarian direction. The news reporter might ask, "How would you find more revenue for education?" Then the Libertarian candidate can say, "I'd like to cut government spending on education instead!"

Libertarians held just over a hundred elected offices nationwide in 2012. Most of these offices are in small jurisdictions, like small city councils and school boards, where it's practical for a candidate to campaign door-to-door and meet lots of voters face-to-face. While Libertarians have won some partisan races (races where they are listed on the ballot as a Libertarian), a majority of the elected Libertarians have been in nonpartisan offices.

I tell people that if you think you have a chance of winning an election, or if you would at least enjoy trying, go for it! Even if you don't win, it will help our cause, and it will be a great experience.

I have to say, I've gotten plenty of grief over the years from Libertarians who criticize me for admitting that Libertarians are likely to lose elections.

They usually say something like, "People won't take a candidate seriously if they aren't running to win," implying that we should never admit we're unlikely to win! Or that I don't care about winning elections, and just want to be part of a debate club where Libertarians argue about what it means to be a perfect Libertarian.

If I believed that saying "I will win" would cause Libertarians to start winning elections, of course I'd do it.

The thing is, the Libertarian Party has been around since 1971, and we've run thousands of candidates who have lost their elections, including lots of candidates who told everyone they were going to win. (Of course, losing elections is not unique to the Libertarian Party. Nearly all other third parties have similar histories of losing to the entrenched Republicans and Democrats.)

I hope things change and Libertarians start winning more elections, and I have personally worked hard to help make that happen.

But most people already know it's unlikely for a Libertarian to win a particular race, and those people need some rationale for supporting Libertarian candidates with their time, donations, and votes. And I think they need something besides "This time it's different—this time I'll win!" They've already heard that many times.

I wish every member of the Libertarian Party would commit to running as a candidate for something—school board, Congress, city council, dogcatcher, State Senator, County Auditor, whatever. Winning elections is something that I hope will happen in the future. But generating publicity, changing the debate, and forcing changes in policy are things that *can* happen *now*.

CHAPTER 16

LIFE CYCLE OF A LIBERTARIAN CAMPAIGN

A "how to" guide for Libertarian candidates is outside the scope of this book. However, I wanted to give an overview of the steps involved. I also want to encourage readers to consider running for office as a Libertarian.

Candidate recruitment. The Libertarian Party recruits many candidates directly by sending out communications to their members and asking them to run for office. Additionally, some people decide to run on their own, and they contact the Libertarian Party to find out how.

Choosing an office. I've seen estimates that there are over 500,000 elected offices in the United States. Most people know about President, U.S. Congress, Governor, and Mayor, but many people don't think about all the local offices—school board, county management, city council, and so on.

Also, many big cities are surrounded by small cities and towns that are easy to forget about. For example, while Austin, Texas has its own city council and school district, many other very small towns are right next to, or completely surrounded by the City of Austin: Lago Vista, Lakeway, Mustang Ridge, Rollingwood, West Lake Hills, Pflugerville, Sunset Valley, and others. Each of those has their own group of elected officials.

Many places have elected positions for local boards such as fire, water, parks, zoning and more. I generally urge people to run for whatever office they want, and also to contact the local Libertarian Party for suggestions.

Running to win, or to promote principles? Some Libertarians run for offices they actually have a chance of winning. Others run campaigns for offices that are not (yet) winnable, but they run to get the message out, and to build and promote the Libertarian Party. Both types of campaigns are rewarding and enjoyable to work on.

Libertarians often argue whether it's more important to run for a small winnable office, or to run an educational campaign for a big office like governor or U.S. Congress. I tell people to do what they prefer.

Running to win. It's not a secret how to win a campaign. Plenty of good books, websites, and organizations explain the basics of how to win an election. You make plans, raise money, maybe hire people, develop a message, put up a website, recruit volunteers, attend events, make promises, place ads, mail postcards, make phone calls, and obvious things like that. Get a "how to run for office" book or hire a consultant if you plan to win.

The easiest campaigns to win are the ones with the smallest number of voters. Candidates can go door-to-door and ask each voter for support, without having to spend much money. Two Libertarian candidates won office in Louisiana in 2012 because they were the only ones who filed to run! No opponents entered the races. Several Libertarians have won races in small districts in Pennsylvania with only one write-in vote. Imagine that—going to the polls, writing in your own name, and then finding out you were elected!

<u>Running to promote Libertarian principles.</u> When it comes to running for something like State Representative or U.S. Congress, where a Libertarian is very unlikely to win, the goal is to get publicity, have fun, and spend just enough money so that you'll feel like running again two years later. I call that an educational or party-building campaign, and I think it's very valuable.

For top-of-ticket offices like U.S. Senator or Governor, the expectations are usually higher than for other educational campaigns. These races are highly visible, so it's good to have an enthusiastic candidate with good libertarian principles and a significant amount of time to devote.

Planning. Once you've decided what to run for and whether you think you can win, it's good to put together an overall plan. A plan should include goals, tasks to complete, team members, a schedule, and a budget. You can find plenty of campaign plan templates in books or on the Internet.

If you are running an educational campaign, the plan can be as simple as you want.

Paperwork. The rules are different in every state. You can spend 40 hours just researching and reading all of the rules for your state. The good news is that most of the paperwork can be very easy if you get help from someone who has run before, or from local or state Libertarian Party leaders who can step you through the process. The paperwork usually involves some sort of candidate application, and possibly a financial disclosure and/or campaign finance registration. When I recruited a record 173 candidates for the Libertarian Party of Texas in 2008, making the paperwork easy for them was my top priority, which was probably why I was able to recruit so many candidates.

Petitions & filing fees. Some offices in some states require you to collect signatures or pay a filing fee to appear on the ballot. Many offices require no filing fee and no petition signatures. If required, the amount of the fee and quantity of signatures vary dramatically, so you'll need to research that for your particular office. For example, you need 125 signatures for House of Delegates in Virginia, but 25,000 to be a candidate for governor in Illinois. Sometimes the Republicans and Democrats also have to get the signatures, like in Virginia, but in states like Illinois, the Republicans and Democrats have exempted themselves. (Real fair, right?)

The Libertarian Party is famous for being the most successful third party in the U.S. for getting candidates onto the ballot, so don't let the fees and petitions intimidate you.

Campaign finance reports. Most candidates, but not all, have to file some kind of campaign finance report. Learning the process can be a pain at first, but once you've filed one it becomes pretty easy. You are basically reporting the name, address, date, amount, and possibly the occupation and employer for the donations you accept. Then you report the date, amount, payee, and purpose of your campaign expenditures. Some candidates appoint a treasurer to handle this paperwork for them.

Getting the Libertarian Party's nomination. This is often a formality, but sometimes nominations are contentious. Occasionally more than one Libertarian wants to run for the same office. In these cases, just like with the Republicans and Democrats, it's up to voters to choose the Libertarian Party nominee. Sometimes the candidates face each other in a primary, but in most states, the two candidates face each other in a convention attended by Libertarian Party activists. Those conventions may have just a few participants, or sometimes up to a hundred, but rarely more than that.

You definitely should talk to the local Libertarian Party about the schedule and procedure for getting the Libertarian Party's nomination. If they know who you are, and you are the only Libertarian Party candidate, it's usually a piece of cake to get the party's nomination. In rare circumstances, you'll have to do some campaigning.

Website and social media. One of the cheapest and most important things a candidate can do is set up a simple website with her name, office, contact info, photo, a short bio, and a few paragraphs about her stances on a few issues. There's an old saying that reporters are lazy, so make it easy for them to report about you. Social media services like Facebook help you reach the public as well.

Issues. Very few voters spend much time reading about candidates, so it's good to have just three issues to highlight. I like to pick issues where the incumbent supported a controversial issue that grew government. Also, while Republicans and Democrats often sound vague and speak out of both sides of their mouths, I encourage Libertarians to be clear and to the point—it gets you noticed more, and voters appreciate a straight talker!

Raising money. Big donors and political action committees typically donate to people they expect to win, because they want political favors in return. If you are not likely to win, then you will probably be funding most of your campaign out of your own pocket and with the support of friends and other local Libertarians.

Brochures, bumper stickers, yard signs. Depending on your budget, you may have to pay for these out of your own pocket (if you want them at all). I once spent $11,000 out of my own pocket on a city council campaign because I wanted every willing volunteer and supporter to have as much promotional stuff as they could use. But it's optional, and don't spend money you can't afford.

Surveys. Once you file the paperwork to be a candidate, many special-interest organizations will probably contact you to complete surveys for them. These surveys are part of the free publicity for low-budget Libertarian campaigns that I've been talking about. The League of Women Voters Guide is one of my favorites.

Candidate forums and debates. Organizations like neighborhood associations, special-interest groups, the League of

Women Voters, and news organizations often host candidate forums and debates. The audiences are often small, but if the press shows up, or if they are televised live, this is your chance to reach thousands of people.

Campaign events. Many campaigns host one or two parties at a house or restaurant. While these usually function as fundraisers, they also serve to recruit, motivate, and thank volunteers.

Get Out The Vote efforts. If you are running a serious campaign, then you may have volunteers making phone calls, sending emails, going door to door, and holding up signs at polling places.

Election night party. On election day, after the polls close, many candidates have some type of election night party. Often many Libertarian candidates have a combined party at one location to watch the election returns come in on television. Whether you win or not, it's cool to see your name on TV!

Things not to worry about:

Hate mail. When I first ran for office, I was expecting lots of people to contact me and argue with me. I quickly learned that hardly anyone does that. I had my name, address, phone, and email posted publicly on a website, but almost no one contacted me out of the blue. I had to make an effort to get people to pay attention. I got several negative emails (which were sometimes quite entertaining), but that was about it. I know candidates for higher offices like Governor or Senator get more of that, but it's usually mild and manageable.

Dirt. Unless you are likely to win a race for something big like Congress, the press just isn't interested in going out and trying to dig up scandalous gossip about you. I'm not going to make this chapter a personal confession, but let's just say I did plenty of things when I was younger that might have made the news if I was a Republican or Democratic candidate for president. But in the campaigns I actually ran, it wasn't an issue.

Libertarian campaigns for office can last anywhere from a couple of months to a couple of years. Most Libertarian Party candidates have full-time jobs, and many have families, so running for office is just a small part-time effort.

Are you ready to run for office? I've run for office five times myself. You can do it too! I think it's a fun and rewarding experience, and so do many other Libertarian candidates.

CHAPTER 17

HOW TO DONATE AND VOLUNTEER

If you want to help the Libertarian Party's efforts, you can volunteer your time, donate money, or both!

I think the very first thing you should do is join the national Libertarian Party for $25. Visit LP.org or call 1-800-ELECT-US to join. Your $25 membership isn't just a donation—it also puts you in the LP membership database so you'll receive printed newsletters and electronic communications. The national LP will forward your information to your state party as well, which may also make it available to your county Libertarian Party chapter. You may find ways to volunteer on your own, but if the local party has your information, they can contact you when specific volunteer opportunities arise.

If you have more to donate, then you need to decide where it makes the most sense to give. If your state or local party contacts you and asks for funds for something worthwhile, then I recommend giving your next $100 or $500 to your local or state affiliate. If your local or state affiliate is not asking you for funds by email or with a fundraising letter, that could be a sign they aren't organized enough to put your funds to good use. If that's the case, donating more to the national Libertarian Party is always helpful. I've been a monthly donor to the national LP for over ten years, a monthly donor to a state affiliate for years, and a donor to county affiliates as well.

It's also good to donate to Libertarian candidates, even the ones who aren't going to win.

Many of the most reliable financial donors are also the best volunteers. But whether or not you are able to donate money, there are many helpful things you can do, and ways to volunteer your time:

Vote Libertarian. Vote for Libertarian candidates in every election. Don't waste your vote on Republicans or Democrats.

Register Libertarian. Thirty-one states allow voters to indicate a political party preference as part of registering, and most of those include Libertarian as an option. Contact your state voter registration authority to see how to change your voter registration to "Libertarian."

Join the Libertarian Party. You can become a dues-paying member as described before, or send an email to members@lp.org to find out how to join for free. Joining the Libertarian Party is different from registering as a Libertarian.

Sign up for newsletters. Visit LP.org, and your state and local websites, and sign up for email newsletters. You'll find out about local events or campaigns you can help with. You may also receive Libertarian Party commentary on current events that you can forward to friends.

Internet and Social Media. Identify yourself as a Libertarian on your personal websites, blogs, and social media accounts like Facebook. Put links to the Libertarian Party websites and to the World's Smallest Political Quiz on your websites and at the bottom of your emails. You'll find lots of lively discussions as well as grassroots organizing efforts and suggestions on practically every social media site. Social media changes rapidly, but at the time of writing this book you'll find lots of Libertarian activity on the social media sites of Facebook, Meetup, Yahoo! Groups, YouTube, Twitter, and LinkedIn.

Bumper stickers and T-shirts. Put a Libertarian bumper sticker on your car. They're great conversation starters in the parking lot, and help show support for the party. T-shirts provide similar publicity. Order them from Libertarian websites. Buy extras and give them away.

Brochures and flyers. Buy some Libertarian brochures (or print your own) and share them with friends or other interested people. Usually around election time you can find candidates or party officials asking for volunteers to distribute flyers in their neighborhood.

World's Smallest Political Quiz. The Advocates for Self-Government offers a business-card-sized version of the World's Smallest Political Quiz. Carry them in your wallet and pull them out when the topic of politics comes up. People enjoy taking The Quiz even if they find out they are not libertarian.

Get others to join. If you find someone who agrees with libertarian positions, ask them to join the Libertarian Party.

Write letters to the editor. Be sure to put the word "Libertarian" in your letters to help build the Libertarian brand. You can find tips for writing letters online.

Call talk radio. Give your point of view and be sure to mention you are a "Libertarian."

Give away Libertarian books. A major reason I wrote this book is because I could not find a good short and simple book about the libertarian political philosophy that also had lots of practical information about the Libertarian Party. I hope you'll buy more copies of this book and share them with friends. You can find many more books by libertarian authors that discuss specific issues in much greater depth.

Libertarian outreach booths. The next time you are at a public event and see anything political, tell yourself "maybe I should have a Libertarian booth here next time." The Advocates for Self-Government has something called an Operation Politically Homeless kit that includes the World's Smallest Political Quiz and other materials. That kit, along with some Libertarian Party brochures and bumper stickers, is about all you need to fill up a table at a public event. I used to ask permission from the local Libertarian Party before setting up a booth. Then I realized I didn't need their permission! I just started paying for the booths out of my own pocket, and I asked for any volunteers that wanted to help me. I've had Libertarian booths or tables at art fairs, county fairs, gun shows, political events, music festivals, and on the lawn of the Texas State Capitol. You hand out literature, get people to take The Quiz, collect people's names and contact information, and then give those names to the Libertarian Party. You can also hand out voter registration cards and ask people to join the Libertarian Party.

Speak at city council meetings. Local and state governments often have opportunities for public comment. I used to enjoy going to Austin City Council or Travis County Commissioner meetings and speaking. I would typically say something like, "My name is Wes Benedict. I'm a Libertarian and I'm against your proposal because…" If the meetings are televised, you might be surprised how many people tell you they saw you on TV.

Volunteer for a campaign. If it's election season, check with the local Libertarian Party to see if any Libertarians are running for office where you live. Candidates need campaign managers, campaign treasurers, and people willing to make phone calls, help with websites, make brochures, organize volunteers, and many other tasks. I want to warn you in advance, though, most Libertarian candidates have busy personal lives. They usually have full-time jobs and families, and they usually aren't millionaires. Libertarian candidates are volunteers who find ways to squeeze in time promoting libertarianism by attending candidate forums, getting publicity, and educating voters. Just because you are ready to volunteer doesn't mean the candidate has a job sitting there ready for you to do. Candidates need volunteers who are patient, flexible, jack-of-all-trades, and reliable. Candidates need low-maintenance volunteers who are ready to do what they are asked when the candidate is ready. When no Libertarian Party candidates needed my help, I have occasionally volunteered for non-Libertarian candidates to get more experience on running campaigns.

Volunteer for your local Libertarian Party. Local Libertarian Party chapters need Chairs, Vice Chairs, Treasurers, Secretaries, newsletter writers, fundraisers, communications directors, webmasters, and plenty more. Most importantly they need people who will go out of their way to be nice, who will be patient, and who will be reliable. Unfortunately, it's pretty common for new people to show up excited, demand rapid improvement, work hard for several weeks, burn themselves out, and then quit without handing over the account passwords. I encourage people to volunteer locally, but work at a pace that is sustainable for the long term. If there is no local Libertarian Party, you can volunteer to start one, or just serve as a local contact. Once you are active with your local chapter, you might also want to serve as a representative to your state party.

Run for office. The biggest way you can help move the Libertarian Party forward is to run for office yourself. If you are considering throwing your hat in the ring, I encourage you to contact your local and state parties, and also the national Libertarian Party, and let them know.

CHAPTER 18

ARE LIBERTARIANS WASTING THEIR VOTES?

The short answer is, no.

Win or lose, every vote for a Libertarian Party candidate sends a message that you are fed up with what the Republicans and Democrats are delivering, and that you want more freedom.

If you support libertarian principles, voting for a Republican or Democrat is a wasted vote. When you vote Republican, you send a message that you condone what Republican politicians do. When you vote Democrat, you send a message that you condone what Democratic politicians do.

When you vote for a Republican or a Democrat, you are saying that you're happy with gigantic government.

People often say if you vote for a Libertarian Party candidate, you are wasting your vote because the Libertarian probably will lose.

Mitt Romney lost his campaign for president. Were all of his votes wasted votes? If voting for a loser means wasting your vote, then I guess every Republican wasted his or her vote. I do know that every *Libertarian* who voted for Mitt Romney wasted his or her vote. Mitt Romney started a plan like Obamacare for Massachusetts, supported the TARP bailouts, and supported all of the American interventions in the Middle East. If you voted for Mitt Romney when you disagreed with his policies, then you wasted your vote because you just encouraged the next Republican candidate to adopt more of the same policies.

If you voted for President Obama but you oppose the Patriot Act, oppose the wars and occupations of Iraq and Afghanistan, and oppose the war on drugs and corporate welfare, then you wasted your vote too.

And guess what? Your vote made no difference in who won the election! The fact is, your vote will probably never decide who wins an election.

Because California is so overwhelmingly Democratic, every informed Democrat and Republican knew Obama would win California. And they all knew Romney would win Texas. Does that mean no one should have voted for Romney in California? No one should have voted for Obama in Texas? Well, millions of people did, because they *wanted to do what they believed in* even though they knew their guy would lose.

Only once in a while, like in 2000 in Florida, is it possible that a few votes might be the deciding factor in a presidential election. But given how horrible George W. Bush turned out to be, would it have mattered much if Gore had been president instead? Gore sounds extreme today as an environmental opportunist and profiteer, but as vice president under Bill Clinton, his policies were almost the same as what Republicans delivered.

I voted for Ross Perot in 1992. I was disgusted with George Bush Senior's tax increases after saying, "Read my lips, no new taxes." I did not expect Perot to win. I did not care who won. But I did not waste my vote. Perot's number one issue was that we needed to cut the deficit. Perot lost, Clinton won, and guess what—for the only time in many decades, Clinton delivered some balanced budgets.

In 1996, I joined the Libertarian Party. Later that year, I voted for Republican Bob Dole for president. I felt really dirty afterwards. I had despised Bob Dole for years because he almost always supported bigger government, yet I voted for him. He lost his election, and I wasted my vote because I rewarded the Republican Party for nominating him, which probably helped George W. Bush get nominated in 2000, McCain in 2008, and Romney in 2012.

People are conformists. Very few strike out on their own and take a stand. When you vote Libertarian, and you tell people about it, you help give others the courage to do the same. When you vote Democrat or Republican, you pour cold water on the courage that may have been flickering in someone else's heart. Libertarians need help and encouragement, not discouragement.

Enough about presidential elections. Did you know that the outcome of most other elections in America are widely known long before election day? Most congressional and state house districts are "safe"—they almost never switch from Democrat to Republican control, or vice versa. I'm not saying there's some kind of conspiracy, but it's usually obvious which party will win because people's voting habits are slow to change. Your vote for a Libertarian in one of those elections will send a message. And if the election is one of the few in America that is actually going to be close between the Democrat and Republican, then your vote for a Libertarian will send a *very loud* message.

I will not be a coward. I will not be a conformist. I will not encourage continuation of the status quo. I will not discourage others who are trying their best to make a difference. I will not let the Democrats and Republicans fool me into thinking the world will end if the other party gets into office. I will not walk out of the voting booth feeling ashamed of what I did. I will vote for what I believe in.

CHAPTER 19

THE LIBERTARIAN MOVEMENT OUTSIDE THE LIBERTARIAN PARTY

The libertarian movement is much bigger than just the Libertarian Party. Many think tanks and other nonprofits promote libertarian ideas and solutions. While many libertarians associate with the Libertarian Party, others choose to work as Republicans or Democrats, remain independent, or stay out of partisan politics and work on specific issues.

As a basis for comparison, here's my attempt to calculate the financial resources of Libertarian Party efforts. The Libertarian National Committee had revenue of about $1.5 million in 2012. I don't have complete data, but based on some reports I've seen, I'd estimate that all 50 Libertarian state affiliates together raise another $500,000 total per year. And I'd guess that all Libertarian county affiliates raise a total of somewhere around $100,000. The Libertarian presidential campaigns raise around $2 million per four-year election cycle, or $500,000 per year. All other Libertarian Party candidates combined raise maybe another $1 million per year. Libertarian Party-supporting political action committees might raise $400,000. There's no official report or central source with all of this information, so I'm making estimates, but this adds up to somewhere around $4 million per year.

Probably the largest and most well-known libertarian think tank is the Cato Institute. I often tell Libertarian Party candidates and activists, we don't need to do a lot of research on every issue that comes up. We don't have the time or resources for that. Just see what the scholars at the libertarian think tanks are saying, and adopt their proposals for your political campaigns or opinion statements.

Cato was founded in 1977 by a former Libertarian Party Chairman, Ed Crane. Cato has a professional, corporate feel to it. Walking through their building you'll see plenty of people wearing suits. Scholars at Cato publish policy research papers from a libertarian perspective on a broad range of topics. Cato also hosts events and has a pretty active website.

Cato had a 2012 budget of $33 million—that's over eight times my estimate for all Libertarian Party entities combined.

I found out about the Cato Institute through the Libertarian Party, and I wrote my first $500 check to Cato shortly after joining the Libertarian Party. Cato started sending me twenty-page reports nearly weekly, which I read and enjoyed at first. After reading several on the topic of Social Security reform, which I already favored, I wasn't sure what I was gaining by reading more reports. I figured I could read every report they wrote until I was a hundred years old and become an expert on every issue. But then I might die, not having changed anything myself. While Cato is good at putting my money to work by paying its employees to generate research documents, it's not clear to me that Cato has an effective way to utilize the time and energy of the average political activist outside of the D.C. area. And probably that is okay.

Occasionally I'll hear comments along the lines of "Libertarians don't get elected—why don't you stop wasting your time and join the

Cato Institute instead." Sometimes I'll even hear of the Libertarian Party being disparaged by Cato staff and interns. I can understand why they feel that way. It's true, Cato scholars are sometimes Harvard professors, while the average Libertarian Party volunteer is not as prestigious.

However, if the Libertarian Party is to be measured by how many Libertarians get elected, then perhaps Cato should be measured by how many of its policies get adopted. The 2011 Cato annual report says, "Over the course of the past year, the federal government has continued to surge in both size and scope to unprecedented levels." Cato is probably the organization that has produced the biggest stack of papers supporting un-adopted libertarian policies.

That doesn't make them a failure in my book. I continue to contribute financially to Cato from time to time, and I find their reports valuable, especially when I'm preparing Libertarian Party messages or position statements on current issues.

Heavily funded think tanks like Cato have their value, but I think the Libertarian Party ultimately shows a bigger "bang for the buck."

The Advocates for Self-Government is another well-known nonpartisan libertarian organization. They developed the famous World's Smallest Political Quiz, which I've covered extensively in this book. The Advocates reported $457,166 in revenue for 2011. They help hundreds (if not thousands) of activists nationwide by providing handouts with the World's Smallest Political Quiz and other materials for outreach booths. They also sell a variety of books and tapes and publish an email newsletter to provide information about the libertarian movement and to help people communicate libertarian ideas.

Based on my years of Libertarian Party activism, I've found that the Advocates for Self-Government and the Cato Institute are the two most useful resources for Libertarian Party efforts.

You can find many other libertarian-leaning organizations linked on Libertarian Party websites. A few of the more common ones are the Reason Foundation (publisher of Reason magazine), Students for Liberty, Ludwig von Mises Institute, Future of Freedom Foundation, Institute for Justice, International Society for Individual Liberty, and the Independent Institute.

Several single-issue advocacy groups have strong libertarian tendencies, such as Antiwar.com, NORML, and Law Enforcement Against Prohibition.

Some libertarians try to promote libertarianism by acting within the Republican and Democratic parties. Congressman Ron Paul is the biggest and most successful example of someone with mostly libertarian principles working inside the Republican Party. Ron Paul was the 1988 Libertarian nominee for president. However, he served as a Republican congressman from Texas multiple terms before and after his 1988 presidential run. Paul ran for president in the Republican primaries in 2008 and 2012. Ron Paul's 2008 campaign raised $34 million, and his 2012 campaign raised $40 million. I don't know how many volunteers helped Ron Paul's campaign, but I would guess hundreds of thousands.

During Ron Paul's campaign people often would ask me, "Instead of helping the Libertarian Party, why don't the Libertarian Party members all help Ron Paul get elected?" I would tell them, "Ron Paul raised over $30 million. Taking money away from the Libertarian Party, which raised only $1.4 million, and giving it to Ron Paul would just be another drop in the bucket and wouldn't get him elected. Besides, I think most Libertarian Party members *have* donated to Ron Paul. I gave over $600 to his campaign. It doesn't have to be either/or. Why don't you give a little to the Libertarian Party?"

I think Ron Paul was the greatest congressman America has had in at least 40 years. He was called "Dr. No" in Congress because he routinely voted against bills that violated the Constitution. He was often the only vote against a bill. Although Ron Paul was a Republican Congressman, he's also a Lifetime Member of the Libertarian Party. He was a special guest speaker at the 2004 and 2006 Libertarian Party of Texas state conventions. I think Ron Paul did more to wake people up to libertarian ideas than any other human being in the twenty-first century.

For some people, and obviously for Ron Paul, it's preferable to work for liberty within the Republican or Democratic parties. However, it's kind of like what I said about Cato: if the Libertarian Party should be measured by election wins, then those efforts should be measured by how much the Republican and Democratic parties have changed. And I haven't seen much change in those parties, unless they've become even more supportive of big government.

I'm not going to try to stop libertarians working to promote liberty through whatever organizations or individual efforts they choose. However, I suspect that working to promote libertarian-leaning Republicans or libertarian-leaning Democrats may end up promoting the overall Republican Party and Democratic Party agendas, which are anti-libertarian. I'm convinced we need a separate party, the Libertarian Party, working free of the entrenched two-party system, to push America towards freedom and away from government control.

CHAPTER 20

FAMOUS LIBERTARIANS

While many actors like Clint Eastwood, Tom Selleck, Kurt Russell, and Drew Carey have called themselves "libertarian" publicly, unfortunately most of them aren't members of the Libertarian Party.

Robert Kraus, Operations Manager of the Libertarian National Committee, told me they once posted Clint Eastwood's picture on the LP.org website—and it wasn't long before Eastwood's people demanded that the photo be removed. I recall laughing pretty hard when I heard that story. I wondered, did Eastwood himself actually know about it and really care, or was it just his publicist doing routine work to protect Eastwood's image? Actually, I was glad to hear people had noticed Eastwood's photo on the website.

People often ask me, "Why don't you get so-and-so to run for president or join the party? He's got millions! People might pay attention!"

Hey—I wish some of those rich and famous people *would* join the Libertarian Party, donate some big bucks, or even run for president! With the national LP having an annual budget of $1.5 million, a celebrity with a million or two to add could make a huge impact.

While the maximum donation allowed to the national Libertarian Party is $32,400 per year (as of 2013), about half the state party affiliates have no maximum limits. Also, PACs can be set up like I describe later in this book, that can accept any size donation—even ten million dollars! Where there's a willing celebrity with time or money, there's a way to put her to work.

While writing this chapter, I came to the realization that I have personally never asked anyone famous to join the Libertarian Party! That could be part of the problem. It's common knowledge that the number one reason people join or donate to a cause is because somebody asked them to. In any case, nothing is stopping you from contacting someone famous and asking them to join the Libertarian Party. If there is someone famous you know personally, try setting up a meeting between the famous person, yourself, and a Libertarian leader. In fact, feel free to set up an appointment between your famous friend and me. I'd be happy to talk with them or even meet with them to discuss the party and options for donating to worthy Libertarian projects. Just beware, I might steer them towards one of my personal projects if I have something going on.

In 2007, a Texas Libertarian candidate, Neill Snider, reached out to Mark Cuban, entrepreneur and owner of the Dallas Mavericks. Neill emailed: "I understand you have mentioned being a Libertarian….The Libertarian Party of Texas is a small organization and you could have a major impact on Texas politics if you get involved."

Mark Cuban is somewhat known for responding to his own emails. The response Neill received from Mark Cuban's email address: "I stay out of politics."

Okay, so that didn't work. But it didn't cost anything and it didn't hurt either. At least Neill tried!

Texas LP state chairman Pat Dixon, who was also my boss at the time, once secured a meeting with John Mackey, CEO of Whole

Foods. (The Federal Election Commission campaign contribution website shows Mackey has contributed several thousand dollars to the Libertarian Party and Libertarian candidates.) Pat invited me to attend. Our goal was to raise money for the Libertarian Party of Texas. At the meeting, Mr. Mackey told us he did not think the Libertarian Party was accomplishing enough and he didn't think it was a good investment, so he wasn't going to donate. That hurt, and I couldn't say he was wrong when looking at the Libertarian Party in general. However, I felt like Pat Dixon and I had accomplished a lot for the Libertarian Party of Texas, compared to other Libertarian Party efforts. We were a pocket of super productivity within the Libertarian Party nationwide, and we had hard data to prove it. I wish we had done a better job of showing that to Mr. Mackey. Lots of Libertarian Party efforts are probably a waste of money, and major donors need to feel confident when they make big donations. I've probably seen a hundred proposals from Libertarians who claimed they were going to do great things—and I had my doubts about most of them. I learned a valuable lesson from John Mackey. It's not enough to have *done* great things. You have to *prove* it, and prove it quickly. And wealthy potential donors didn't get wealthy by falling for every pie-in-the-sky proposal that crosses their desk. They know that many projects, and many people, are not worth investing in, with or without a slick presentation.

American blues rock guitarist and singer Jimmie Vaughan is a Libertarian Party member. Based out of Austin, Texas, he's the older brother of the late musician Stevie Ray Vaughan. Jimmie Vaughan has not only contributed financially, he performed live at the 2004 national Libertarian Party convention in Atlanta. He's also performed for other good political events in Austin, including one for the Libertarian Party of Texas. I guess I can say Jimmie Vaughan is the one Libertarian celebrity I've actually spoken with several times. He has always been very friendly.

An Internet search for "famous libertarians" brings up hundreds of celebrities, writers, CEOs, economists, and others. The Advocates for Self-Government maintains a list of libertarian celebrities and VIPs. Economists include Friedrich Hayek, Ludwig von Mises, Milton Friedman, Murray Rothbard, and Walter Block. Tommy Chong, most famous for the *Cheech and Chong* movies and marijuana legalization efforts, is listed there. Trey Parker, co-creator of the animated series *South Park*, is also listed. For the record, I'm a big *South Park* fan. (While the shows are full of gross and juvenile humor, they often contain libertarian themes.)

Comedian and magician Penn Jillette actually sat down to help produce videos promoting the Libertarian Party.

Comedian Doug Stanhope attended the 2008 Libertarian National Convention in Denver. Unfortunately, he was attending as an upset Libertarian Party constituent, criticizing the party for its choice of presidential nominee. Sometimes comedians can be the harshest critics.

News personalities John Stossel and Judge Andrew Napolitano are well-known for their libertarian political views, but are not members of the Libertarian Party as far as I know. I imagine that many people, perhaps for ethical, business, legal, or other personal reasons, choose not to join the Libertarian Party even if they have libertarian views, and even if they like the Libertarian Party.

PayPal founder Peter Thiel and Cypress Semiconductor CEO TJ Rodgers are often labeled libertarian in the media, as are many other CEOs. One wealthy banker, who sometimes makes the news, has given tens of thousands to the Libertarian Party.

I tend to be wary of talk radio hosts who call themselves libertarians. In 2010, I was working as the executive director of the Libertarian Party in Washington, D.C. I wrote in an email broadcast to roughly 100,000 subscribers that "Radio host Neal Boortz has been booted from our St. Louis National Convention speaker lineup.

On April 2, Boortz told his listeners that voters should not support third parties in the 2010 and 2012 elections, in order to get Republicans elected."

I was subsequently scolded by my boss for sending that, but I get really irritated when someone who used to say "vote Libertarian" changes tune and starts saying vote Republican or vote Democrat. I can understand supporting Ron Paul, but Boortz was not supporting Ron Paul. He was calling for people to support any Republican besides Ron Paul for president, and to support all other Republicans up and down the ballot. I don't regret calling attention to Boortz's "boot." He has some libertarian views, but he turned into a warmonger, even though it's foolish wars that are most responsible for wasting Americans' money, taking away our civil liberties, and inspiring more people to become terrorists. Some celebrities we're better off without.

Talk radio and television personality Glenn Beck sometimes calls himself a libertarian. Quite a few prominent libertarians, like Students For Liberty's Alexander McCobin, have asked Glenn Beck to stop calling himself a libertarian because he pollutes the libertarian brand. Glenn Beck has a long history of supporting un-libertarian things like the Patriot Act, the occupations of Iraq and Afghanistan, and, perhaps most surprisingly, President George Bush's 2008 Troubled Asset Relief Program—the bank bailouts that ignited the 2008 Tea Party movement. Glenn Beck and some of his fans sometimes call Libertarians "purists" or "extremists" for refusing to embrace self-labeled libertarians like him. But Glenn Beck not only has a history of opposing Libertarian Party candidates, he has even supported establishment big-government Republicans like Mitt Romney over Ron Paul for President, and Rick Perry over the less offensive Republican Debra Medina for Texas Governor. I don't know for sure what motivates Glenn Beck. Many libertarians call him a neo-conservative pawn. Perhaps he's ignorant. Perhaps he's motivated primarily by his for-profit ventures and finds he's able to maximize his profits by wrapping his neo-conservatism in libertarian packaging. Whatever his motivations, I think when Glenn Beck calls himself a libertarian, the net effect is to confuse the public into thinking libertarian and conservative are the same thing, and he probably gets some libertarians to vote for Republicans instead of Libertarian Party candidates. For all of my differences with Neal Boortz, at least he had the courage to say "vote for Libertarian Party candidates" on the air for many years. I think Glenn Beck is stuck on the dead-end path of voting Republican no matter what, totally in denial that Republican and Democratic politicians are both leading America in the same wrong direction at approximately the same speed. Glenn Beck could never admit that Republicans Ronald Reagan and George Bush I & II grew government faster than Bill Clinton. Beck is too blinded by his hatred of Democrats, and too easily fooled by Republican rhetoric, to see reality. When Glenn Beck stands up and says publicly he's voting for Libertarian Party candidates, or at least voting against most of the establishment politicians, perhaps then he will have earned the badge of libertarian (or even a Libertarian with a capital L). Until then, he's just exercising his First Amendment right to call himself whatever he wants, as wrong as that might be.

Okay, enough about Glenn Beck. Sorry for the rant.

On a lighter note, is the king of conspiracy theorists, Alex Jones, a libertarian? In 2002 I ran for Travis County Commissioner as the Libertarian Party nominee. Travis is the county that mostly contains Austin, Texas, home of Alex Jones. Back then, I was not really familiar with conspiracy theories or jargon. Terms like New World Order, Illuminati, Trilateral Commission, Rothschilds, and Bilderbergers didn't mean much to me. In any case, I proceeded to launch attacks against my Republican opponent in the race. And "attacks" is probably an exaggeration, because I only spent about $1,500 on my whole campaign. It turns out my Republican opponent was one of Alex Jones's producers, and they didn't like what I was saying. I got a personal call from my opponent, and I could hear Alex Jones berating me in the background. To make a long story short, my relationship with Alex Jones did not start off well. But before long, I grew to appreciate Alex Jones, even if I didn't always agree with what he was saying or doing.

Alex Jones has fairly libertarian political views. I think he sometimes sees grand conspiracies where I might simply see government and big business misbehaving predictably. Nevertheless, I like the fact that Alex Jones causes people to question what government and others tell us. He's very entertaining most of the time, and I wouldn't want Alex Jones to stop being Alex Jones.

While we're on the topic of conspiracy theorists, former professional wrestler and Minnesota Governor Jesse Ventura has been very friendly and helpful to the Libertarian Party. For one thing, he proved that a third-party candidate can win a governorship. Ventura was the 1998 Reform Party candidate for governor who shocked the establishment by winning against a Republican and Democrat. In 2011, Ventura told me he would be willing to be the Libertarian Party candidate for vice president if Ron Paul would switch to the Libertarian Party and be our presidential nominee. That never happened, but in 2012, Jesse Ventura went on to promote Libertarian nominee Gary Johnson for president. Governor Ventura agreed to appear in three videos produced by Libertarian Action Super PAC (LASPAC), which promoted Gary Johnson. (LASPAC was a Super PAC I co-founded to promote Gary Johnson's Libertarian campaign for president.) Ventura appeared at official Gary Johnson events as well. Ventura is not completely libertarian in his political views, but he's very good on many issues, particularly those related to civil liberties.

So far I've listed several men. Where are all the famous women? Not in the Libertarian Party, unfortunately. Most of the time when

I've looked at membership statistics, donation sources, and when I've looked around the room at Libertarian Party meetings, usually it's mostly male. It seems like the Libertarian Party tends to attract males more, but there are a lot of women too, and there have been some very notable women in the libertarian movement outside the LP.

Ayn Rand, the founder of the Objectivist movement, is sometimes credited with being a libertarian. However, she probably rolls over in her grave every time someone calls her a libertarian, because she claimed she hated the Libertarian Party and libertarianism in general when she was alive. Ayn Rand wrote the 1957 novel *Atlas Shrugged*, which many credit as being the most influential book in their lives. Many libertarians cite *Atlas Shrugged* as a reason for adopting libertarian principles. Objectivism and libertarianism are similar in some ways. At the risk of invoking the ire of orthodox Objectivists, I'll say that one main difference between Objectivism and libertarianism is that Objectivists think it's moral to be self-centered and immoral to be altruistic, whereas libertarians mostly want government to leave you alone, and that means free to be as self-centered or altruistic as you choose. In any case, whether Ayn Rand would like it or not, I read her book, and it did make me more libertarian.

Feminists Naomi Wolf and Camille Paglia are sometimes noted for having libertarian views, particularly on social issues. I could list quite a few lesser-known women who are libertarians, or some famous women who are occasionally noted for having libertarian views on some things (like Angelina Jolie), but the fact remains, women are underrepresented in the Libertarian Party. Some people blame the Libertarian men for repelling women from the Libertarian Party. I object to such insults! Nevertheless, if it takes recruiting Brad Pitt or Justin Bieber into the party—or perhaps I've got it backwards—if it takes recruiting Madonna or Rihanna into the Libertarian Party to attract more women, I'm for it.

CHAPTER 21

LIBERTARIAN INFIGHTING

I thought about using this book to expose some of the most offensive people in the Libertarian Party and to settle some scores with people who have done me wrong. But then I thought, that's exactly the kind of stuff I want to stop!

The Libertarian Party certainly suffers from lots of infighting. Instead of fighting for freedom, or against Republicans and Democrats, too many Libertarians fight with each other. My advice is, avoid infighting.

I've often heard that the Internet made organizing Libertarians easier. In some ways, it has. Sending emails or posting social networking notices are quick and usually free, compared to sending printed mail newsletters and making phone calls. However, along with making things easier, the Internet seems to have made people ruder. People who are usually polite in person can write some of the meanest emails.

Many Libertarian Party groups are highly active with internal fighting and bickering. It seems to happen very frequently all around the country. If you get involved in Libertarian activities, I encourage you to go out of your way to be nice to your colleagues—a few notches nicer than you think is necessary. Pretend if you have to. It can be contagious. And when someone does something that offends you, let it roll off your back most of the time. There's something inherently explosive and implosive about Libertarian affiliates. It takes hard work to be able to stick together and work together. When you can't work together, I encourage you to find ways to work separately, rather than fighting against each other. Libertarians can fight over just about everything. Some of the big things are strategy, marketing, the platform, candidates, party officers, what to work on, how to spend money, and how radical or moderate to be. Of course, Libertarians can also fight about things like font styles on brochures, or what exactly Thomas Jefferson meant when he said so-and-so in 1776.

To be fair, this is not just a Libertarian issue. All political organizations, especially those made up of volunteers, tend to fight internally a lot.

I'm reminded of some advice that was given to a Maryland State Convention by a former executive director of the Libertarian Party, Paul Jacob. Mr. Jacob presented ten commandments for liberty activists. Number one was "Do something." The most important thing is to take action. No one knows for sure what will work. His number two piece of advice was, "Don't stop others from doing something." Spend your energy doing more of your preferred type of activism, rather than trying to stop others from defending liberty in their preferred way.

It's not easy working on a Libertarian Party committee. The people on Libertarian Party committees, and the members who attend meetings, are volunteers with diverse professional backgrounds and varying personalities. It's hard to fire a volunteer. Furthermore, many Libertarian Party officers are technically elected officials. You can't fire most of them, just like you can't fire your

Congressman or City Council, except at election time. I encourage patience and polite behavior when volunteering with the Libertarian Party.

One advantage of running for office is that you can manage your campaign and your staff any way you want to. Additionally, campaigns for office give Libertarian volunteers something useful to work on, instead of just sitting around arguing with each other. I've seen lots of quality campaigns develop quickly to the point where they raise more money and have more volunteers than a whole county or state Libertarian Party chapter. If you like to do things "your way," I suggest running for office. As the candidate, you are the CEO and Chairman of your campaign. You can say anything you want, print anything you want, pick whatever colors you want for your yard signs, and recruit or fire any volunteers or staff that you want. Of course, if you want to get a lot done, you'll need to delegate most of those activities.

In the following chapter, I'll discuss how working through PACs can be a great way to organize and get things done, especially as an alternative to a party committee that is bogged down by infighting.

CHAPTER 22

LIBERTARIAN PACS: WHERE MILLIONAIRES SHOULD DONATE

Millionaires and billionaires can work around many contribution limits by giving to Political Action Committees (PACs) that accept unlimited contributions. Additionally, PACs allow people who agree on certain strategies to work efficiently doing things the way they want to, rather than having to spend time fighting with others over what strategies to pursue. PACs are usually privately organized, unlike party committees, which are usually democratically elected (by law).

Libertarian Party committees at all levels, and certainly at the state level, are notorious throughout the U.S. for spending lots of time on internal arguments and battles. The infighting leaves less energy and fewer opportunities for productive work, and drives away lots of people. It's not that there are bad people on those committees. It's just inherent to the way the people on those committees are selected. And it's not a problem unique to Libertarians—Democrats, Republicans, and others face the same internal struggles.

Representatives of the party committees are democratically elected by members. Those committee representatives don't all agree on what to do. For example, some may want to promote candidates for local races that are easier to win, while others may want to promote candidates for high offices like governor, because of the sizable amount of free press coverage a candidate for governor typically gets. Committee representatives may spend hundreds of hours fighting over which path to take, even though they possibly could have accomplished both strategies in the time they spent debating. It's common for party committees to have long meetings where they spend literally hours debating over tiny details.

Towards the end of my tenure as executive director of the Libertarian Party of Texas, a man approached me and said something along the lines of, "What could the Libertarian Party do if it had a million dollars?"

Unfortunately, I had already given notice long ago that I was resigning from the Texas LP, and my resignation date was just ten days away. And now, finally, somebody with real money wanted to donate. My timing sucks!

One of my thoughts was that if he gave a million dollars to the Libertarian Party of Texas, the Libertarian Party of Texas would spend two million dollars' worth of time and money fighting over it. The donor went ahead and made a small donation to the Libertarian Party of Texas.

After leaving the executive director position, I approached the donor with the idea of funding a separate PAC to help the Libertarian Party and its candidates in Texas. However, the donor did not choose to go for it at that time.

Later, the donor decided to make large contributions to the LP Texas and a couple of PACs set up by newer activists in Texas. That was exciting and good (but to be honest, I was a bit jealous, because I was no longer in Texas and wasn't part of the projects). But I noticed that the large donation to the state party led to a lot of infighting (as I expected), both before and after the money was spent. And in my opinion, the money was spent ineffectively.

Setting up PACs is nothing new. Republicans and Democrats have done it for many years. Even Libertarians have set up several PACs over the years with varying levels of success.

Since leaving my position with the national Libertarian Party at the end of 2011, I've set up two PACs, with most of the funding coming from the donor mentioned before. Persistence paid off. While I think the PACs I founded have done good work, I'd say the jury's still out on whether those PACs have delivered enough results. Time will tell. If they do well enough, I expect donors to keep funding them. PACs represent an entrepreneurial way to promote the Libertarian Party and its candidates.

Rules for PACs vary greatly from state to state, with separate rules for federal candidates. The details are outside the scope of this book. Additionally, there are many other types of organizations, such as educational 501(c)(3) nonprofits, that can be set up to benefit the libertarian movement.

In general, I think it's good to donate to whatever organization you think is delivering the best results. Sometimes that means giving to the national LP, sometimes to your state or county party, sometimes to a great candidate. When $20,000, $100,000, or $1 million is involved, it may make the most sense to pair up large donors with like-minded hard workers, and form PACs to promote Libertarian Party efforts from the outside. When a party governing committee gets bogged down with infighting, forming a PAC is a good way to sidestep that infighting.

I'll be doing my best to deliver results with any PACs I operate. I hope others see my work and create even better Libertarian PACs! The Libertarian Party movement needs organizations competing to deliver the biggest bang for the buck, just like the free market where businesses compete to deliver the best value to their customers.

CHAPTER 23

HOPE FOR THE FUTURE

Democratic and Republican politicians try to make it sound like they are very different from each other, but on all the big issues of our time, they deliver the same results.

It takes Libertarians to point out that Republicans supported the 2003 Medicare expansion, the No Child Left Behind Act, the 2008 TARP bailouts, the GM and Chrysler bailouts, subsidies for ethanol, and lots of other government programs.

It takes Libertarians to point out that Democrats violate civil liberties just as much as Republicans. Democrats supported the invasions of Afghanistan and Iraq, the Patriot Act, continuing the war on drugs, invasions of our privacy, and drone bombings in Pakistan and elsewhere.

America can do better. Libertarians are showing the way.

The best way most people can help is to run for office as a Libertarian. Win or lose, every vote for a Libertarian sends a message. People notice large vote totals for Libertarians even if they don't win their elections. You can go to protests or political meetings and be another voice in the crowd, or you can run for office and amplify your voice a thousand times with free media coverage and publicity.

The Libertarian Party has done some things well, and other things not so well. The biggest success has been the publicity for important issues our candidates get when they run for office. I think the biggest failure has been the number of people who give up after one election cycle, even when their efforts are showing growth. No huge successful business or movement was built overnight. Not even the American Revolution.

Losing elections is not a wasted effort, and not a reason to quit. The Cato Institute publishes thousands of policy papers, almost none of which get implemented, but they don't give up. How much worse might things be if organizations like the Cato Institute and the Libertarian Party didn't expose big government and explain how freedom benefits everyone?

When I consider how all of the Libertarian Party affiliates and candidates added up together nationwide raise about $4 million per year (about the same revenue as two typical McDonald's restaurants), I realize America has not really given the Libertarian Party a try.

There are hundreds of billionaires and many thousands of multi-millionaires in the United States. Many of those wealthy individuals have libertarian views. Most of those individuals could double the size of the Libertarian Party overnight if they wanted to. With the PACs I've set up, I've shown that millionaires will invest generously in Libertarian Party activities when they see productive work and are simply asked to contribute. I will try to do more of that to help build the party, but I hope more Libertarians will also go out and try it on their own.

Will America adopt libertarian principles in the future?

I think it's possible. We've been losing on some fronts, but winning on others.

I don't know if the Libertarian Party's efforts will successfully reverse the trend of ever-expanding government in the United States.

I *can* say that I tried. You can too. If enough of us try, that will make our future a lot brighter.

I hope you'll join me and the Libertarian Party in our fight for freedom today. We need your help. Please go to one of the many Libertarian websites today, and make a generous donation, or sign up to volunteer.

ABOUT THE AUTHOR

Wes Benedict joined the Libertarian Party in 1996. From July 17, 2009 to December 31, 2011, he served as the executive director of the Libertarian National Committee in the Libertarian Party's headquarters in Washington, D.C. He previously served as the executive director of the Libertarian Party of Texas. There he broke records and made Texas one of the best performing state Libertarian Party chapters. He recruited a record 173 LP candidates for office in Texas for the November 2008 elections, which was 29 percent of the nationwide LP total. In 2012 he co-founded the Libertarian Booster PAC to help promote Libertarian Party candidates entrepreneurially. Mr. Benedict holds an MBA from the University of Michigan and a Mechanical Engineering degree from the University of Texas. He has previously bought and sold a kitchen and bath countertop manufacturing business, and he has worked as a management consultant for PricewaterhouseCoopers and a manufacturing engineer for 3M Company.

Made in the USA
Lexington, KY
18 January 2014